Translation as Advocacy

Language Acts and Worldmaking

Series Editors: Professor Catherine Boyle, Professor Debra Kelly, Dr Ana de Medeiros and Dr Carlos Montoro

This book series takes its name from the research, teaching, learning and public engagement carried out by Language Acts and Worldmaking (**www.languageacts.org**). By worldmaking we mean the power of language, as a material and historical force, to shape the ways we construct our personal, local and transnational identities and therefore how we live and make our worlds. Furthermore, language learning is key to understanding how societies are structured and governed and to empowering culturally aware and self-reflective citizens. Put simply, Language Acts and Worldmaking explores how the languages we use affect the way we think and feel about ourselves, about other people and about the world around us.

The series expands this work at national and international levels by inviting the contributions of researchers, teachers, learners and users of diverse languages across the world. The aim is twofold: to challenge widely held views about language learning as a neutral instrument of globalization and to innovate and transform language research, teaching and learning, together with Modern Languages as an academic discipline, by foregrounding its unique form of cognition and critical engagement.

The aims of the Language Acts and Worldmaking book series are to:

- propose new ways of bridging the gaps between those who teach and research languages and those who learn and use them in everyday contexts from the professional to the personal;
- put research into the hands of wider audiences (teachers, students of all ages, communities, those generally interested in language and culture);
- share a philosophy, policy and practice of language teaching and learning which turns research into action;
- provide the research, experience and data to enable informed debates on current issues and attitudes in language learning, teaching and research;
- share knowledge across and within all levels and experiences of language learning and teaching;
- showcase exciting new work that derives from different types of community activity and is of practical relevance to its audiences;
- disseminate new research in languages that engages with diverse communities of language practitioners.

The main focus of each volume differs. Some deal with current issues in language research, teaching and learning. Others primarily engage with practical aspects of language teaching, learning and research at varied educational levels or in contexts outside formal structures of institutions. Some focus on research and the academic discipline of Modern Languages and those disciplines most closely allied to it, for example Linguistics, Cultural Studies, History, and so on. All volumes are underpinned by research while maintaining a balance with experiences of the application of research findings.

Titles in the series:

Language Debates
Language Acts and Worldmaking
Multilingual Narratives of a Pandemic

Translation as Advocacy

Perspectives on Practice, Performance and Publishing

Edited by Catherine Boyle and Sarah Maitland

JOHN MURRAY LANGUAGES

lānguāgë âçts and worldmåkiṅg

First published by John Murray Languages in 2024
An imprint of John Murray Press

1

A CIP catalogue record for this title is available from the British Library

Trade Paperback ISBN 9781399816144
eBook ISBN 9781399816151

Typeset in Univers by 10.5/14 by Integra Software Services Pvt. Ltd., Pondicherry, India

Printed and bound in Great Britain by Clays Ltd, Elcograf S.p.A.

John Murray Press policy is to use papers that are natural, renewable and recyclable products and made from wood grown in sustainable forests. The logging and manufacturing processes are expected to conform to the environmental regulations of the country of origin.

John Murray Press
Carmelite House
50 Victoria Embankment
London EC4Y 0DZ

Nicholas Brealey Publishing
Hachette Book Group
Market Place, Center 53, State Street
Boston, MA 02109, USA

languageacts-worldmaking.com
John Murray Press, part of Hodder & Stoughton Limited
An Hachette UK company

Contents

Contributors

Tom Boll, University of East Anglia, UK

Catherine Boyle, King's College London, UK

Katie Brown, University of Exeter, UK

Charlotte Coombe, co-founder, Translators Aloud YouTube channel

Beverley Costa, Birkbeck, University of London, UK, and University of Reading, UK

Tina Kover, co-founder, Translators Aloud YouTube channel

Sarah Maitland, Goldsmiths, University of London, UK

Teresa Murjas, University of Reading, UK

Sophie Stevens, Institute of Languages, Culture and Societies, University of London, UK

Lisha Xu, University of Edinburgh, UK

Foreword: translation and/as advocacy

Catherine Boyle and Sarah Maitland

What does it mean to advocate – in translation, *for* translation, *through* translation? What does advocacy look like for those who do the translating or for those whose work is translated? To what extent is translation itself a form *of* advocacy? These 'what' questions are the driving force for each of the contributions in this collection. Yet, as you will see, answers to these questions do not come easily because whenever we talk about advocacy in connection with the academic theorization, professional practice and/or pedagogy of translation, prepositions always proliferate – *in, for, through* – and this is clear across the small but growing number of popular and scholarly works to have addressed the topic so far.

Advocacy is something that translation researchers advocate *for* (see, for example, von Flotow and Josephy-Hernández, 2018, who call for increased levels of gender awareness and sensitivity in audiovisual translation professional practice) or which takes place *in* particular contexts of public life where cultural encounter is present (see Blackledge and Creese, 2020, on multilingual interactional encounters between private citizens negotiating complex bureaucratic systems and the advice workers charged with supporting them). It is also something that trained language professionals *do*, as in the case of bilingual health advocates who educate providers about the needs of culturally sensitive healthcare provision and ensure that patients and healthcare workers can communicate in a common language.[1]

When it comes to the conditions of a given translation contract, it is something that professional translators call *for*, as in the successful petition by Veronica Liu of Word Up Community

[1] Such as the Barts Bilingual Health Advocacy and Interpreting Service in London, UK.

Bookshop and the Dominican Writers Association, which together called for a Dominican–American Spanish translation of Angie Cruz's *Dominicana* rather than the more common model of translation into Standard Peninsular Spanish.[2] In the words of Antonia Lloyd-Jones (in Gasper Bye, n.d.), meanwhile, advocacy means acting as a 'cultural ambassador' for the literature the translator translates, supporting the writers of that literature and the literary agents from the places where that literature originates to find publishers and promote their work in translation. Across all these interventions on the topic, advocacy points to the things that go *into*, *around*, *in advance of* and *after* the act of translation.

The term 'advocacy' as we know it in English today comes by way of the Medieval Latin *advocatia*, which itself is a derivative of *advocare* – to 'call', 'summon' or 'invite'. Advocacy owes its definitional diversity – the proliferation of prepositions – to the multifarious ways in which a call for change in or involving translation can both be made and received. Together, these calls represent a summons to reflection – on the causes and effects of translation – and an invitation to consider different ways of thinking and being – through and thanks to it.

This collection offers eight such invitations, spanning extended contributions from five practising translator-academics, one interview with the founders of a translation-focused YouTube channel, one full-length work of theatre translation, and an afterword from the founder of the Out of the Wings Collective and Principal Investigator of the Language Acts and Worldmaking project. Eight forms of advocacy in all and eight ways in which advocacy is either present in particular contexts of existing translation or is otherwise argued for in contexts yet to be materialized. In 'Advocacy as legal argument: the judicial interpretive task of the translator', Sarah Maitland invites readers

[2] As Tiffany Troy (2021) reports, one of the consequences of the practice by American literary publishers of selling the Spanish world rights to large-scale publishers based in Spain is that the translations that are produced through such contracting processes tend to be wrought in Standard Peninsular Spanish. The campaign by Liu and the Dominican Writers Association was successful: Seven Stories Press was able to purchase the translation rights, and the translation by Dominican translator, writer and Spanish lecturer Kianny N. Antigua was published in 2021.

to go on a journey of philosophical reflection on the interpretive role of the translator as an 'advocate' – in the legal sense – for both the text of the translation and the author whose work is translated. Analogous to the dialectical processes of interpretation and argumentation, understanding and explanation that accompany the judicial process, the complex task of translation requires the translator to make a judgement and to defend that stance transparently in the court of public opinion. As a mode of *doing* that both requires and gives rise to modes of *thinking*, translation exists at the nexus of theory and practice, and this is reflected in a deliberate interweaving across the structure of the collection of critical reflection with the needs and opportunities of concrete translation contexts.

With '*Between*', which we present in its entirety, Beverley Costa and Teresa Murjas model precisely one such context – in the guise of a multilingual play written collaboratively by members of UK-based performance company Around the Well and featuring stories rooted in the real-life experiences of public service interpreters.

In 'Advocating for translations in languages education', Katie Brown locates the space of advocacy within the higher education classroom, where, in a context of language learning, translation emerges as an important tool in the development of critical understanding of one's own language and culture in relation to another. By looking not only at linguistic questions but also at the whole process of moving a text from one audience to another, she argues, the Modern Languages classroom can facilitate debates fundamental to the process of intercultural understanding. Through a case study drawn from her own teaching work in a university setting, she demonstrates how an awareness of translation, including the process which leads to publication, can enhance and expand students' critical thinking about the way they read texts and open up new perspectives on the contribution that literature makes in the target context of the UK. Lisha Xu and Tom Boll each take a historical perspective to consider the advocacy work of translators in the first and second halves of the twentieth century.

In 'Advocacy and collaboration; Stanley Burnshaw's *The Poem Itself*', Boll takes the editorial production process of Burnshaw's 1964 primer in poetic modernism as the starting point for reflection on a form of advocacy performative of Burnshaw's own interpretive stance – with regard not only to the anthology's selection of poems (in French, German, Spanish, Portuguese and Italian, from the previous 150 years) but also to the forms of collaboration with individual contributors (translators, associate editors) and publishing institutions through which the publication would be filtered.

In 'Advocacy and recognition: S. I. Hsiung, a translator of the Chinese diaspora', Xu argues that in this literary figure of the early decades of the twentieth century, and in his translations of Peking Opera in particular, struggles for recognition and more equitable forms of cultural encounter are embodied. Here, advocacy emerges in the condition of cultural in-betweenness experienced by the diasporic translator and which gives rise to a fruitful disruption of the status quo.

With 'Advocating intercultural dialogue through translating artist-activist practice', Sophie Stevens introduces the notion of the 'teacher-translator-academic' as an advocate for translation as a mode of enhanced critical inquiry on the part of students and, through a case study of translation in linguistically and culturally embedded contexts encompassing artist-activist performance practice and hashtags and slogans associated with the feminist movement in Uruguay, argues for a pedagogical approach that embraces the decentring possibilities of classroom translation methods that focus not just on the *product* of translation process but also on the expansion of horizons that comes with the *doing* of translation practice. Together, Stevens and Brown show the significant contribution that an understanding of translation methods can make to university-level study and how including translation on the curriculum for a range of subjects can initiate new lines of inquiry, research and professional practice.

In 'Translators Aloud: advocating for translation, translations and translators', Katie Brown presents an interview with the founders of Translators Aloud, a YouTube channel hosting videos of translators reading from their work, whether published or seeking a publisher. The channel was started by translators Charlotte Coombe and Tina Kover in May 2020 and features more than 300 translators reading from works originally published in or translated into 45 different languages. In the words of Kover, Translators Aloud works to counteract 'not just the tendency of larger publishers or the reading public to overlook the contribution of translation, but the tendency that many translators themselves have to be extremely self-effacing, to downplay their own role in the world of publishing and as creative artists'. Through a cascading flow of advocacy operationalized on their YouTube digital platform, the objects of advocacy become both the translators to whom Coombe and Kover have given voice *and* the translated works, together with their boutique publishers, which the translators showcase through their own contributions.

References

Blackledge, A. and Creese, A. (2020) Recontextualisation and advocacy in the translation zone. *Text & Talk*, 41 (1). DOI: https://doi.org/10.1515/text-2019-0123.

Flotow, L. von and Josephy-Hernández, D. (2018) Gender in audiovisual translation studies: Advocating for gender awareness, in Pérez-González, L. (ed), *The Routledge Handbook of Audiovisual Translation*. London: Routledge.

Gasper Bye, S. (n.d.) The translator as advocate. Available from: https://web.archive.org/web/20220702055727/https://www.themantle.com/literature/translator-advocate (Accessed: 1 March 2023).

Troy, T. (2021) ICYMI: Translation & advocacy: Just translation isn't enough. *Columbia Journal*, 6 February. Available from: www.columbiajournal.org/articles/2021-icymi-translation-amp-advocacy-just-translation-isnt-enough (Accessed: 1 March 2023).

1

Advocacy as legal argument: the judicial interpretive task of the translator

Sarah Maitland

Overview

We tend to think of advocates as people who argue publicly in favour of a particular cause. In jurisprudence, professional advocates champion the case of a particular person or legal entity before a court or tribunal. In both conceptualizations, advocacy is about taking up a voice on behalf of someone who is absent or whose voice has been silenced. In that intimate moment that characterizes the act of reading, the texts we read, consider and later translate are also silent, just as their authors are absent from the proceedings. It is the translator who must advocate for both the author *and* the text.

Focusing on the translation of the dramatic works of nineteenth-century Cuban-Spanish Romantic writer Gertrudis Gómez de Avellaneda, this chapter is a meta-reflection on what it means for the translator to advocate for the meanings they construct within the text-for-translation. I argue that the dialectical processes of interpretation and argumentation, understanding and explanation, that accompany the complex task of translation succeed in geolocating the translator within the time and space of reading. Advocacy emerges as a profound investment in the text as the site of the clues we need to understand it and, if we are lucky, ourselves.

Introduction

We tend to think of advocates as people who argue publicly in favour of a particular cause. In UK government parlance, they are often known as *tsars* – people who have been granted special powers to address identified problems in society by making recommendations in response to a particular need. We might view them simply as people's champions. In jurisprudence, professional advocates champion the cause of private individuals or established legal entities by pleading their case before a court or tribunal. They, too, use reasoned argument to make public their support of another. Think of the *counsellor at law*, who advises clients on how to proceed within a given set of legal circumstances, or the *public defender*, appointed to represent those who cannot reasonably represent themselves. Here, as in the political realm, *representation* is understood as a discourse that is asserted on behalf of constituencies who does not have the opportunity, or the power, to speak for themselves. Whether in law or in civil society, it seems, advocacy is about interceding for the sake of another. Of course, not all advocates intercede in the same ways and not everyone agrees with the approach they may take. Advocates must be prepared to justify their stance when questioned. This is precisely what legal advocates do when they argue their case in response to contrary views mounted by opposing counsel. The space of advocacy is thus a relational space, for it takes place on the plane of *debate* and is shaped only *in response* – to a status quo to be supported or rejected.

Underlying every act of advocacy is a dialogic of argumentation, for it implies, above all, an exchange of (sometimes diverging) views accompanied by a rationale for the opinions being expressed. The space of advocacy is therefore also one of contestation for it crystallizes only in the absence of agreement and in the presence of a conflict. At stake in this conflict is the articulation of a position in the face of uncertainty. Through debate and deliberation, uncertainty is ended with the rendering of a decision. In a trial, which is merely the codified form of the broader phenomenon of conflict (Ricoeur, 2000, p. 130), everything is up for determination – not just the putative facts of the case but also what counts as a relevant fact within it. These facts do not exist as objective truths to be apprehended; they are positions to be taken with respect to the conflict at hand.

Viewed from this perspective, the trial is a drama in which the major players must judge for themselves, and on behalf of those they represent, the significance for the case that each fact holds. Since that which is deemed significant is a question hotly contested, the facts of the trial are, in Ricœur's terms, 'charged with meaning, hence interpreted' (2000, p. 123). Four interlinked terms have so far made an appearance and each plays an important role in the unfolding drama: uncertainty, conflict, meaning and interpretation. The principle of uncertainty surrounds the facts of the case; the meaning of the facts of the case is to be decided by the advocating parties to the conflict, and because meaning does not speak for itself, the sense, content and import of the facts of the case must be imputed and defended, which is to say, *judged*. To 'judge' within this setting is to opine. But since opinions must be expressed *about* something, before engaging in an act of judgement one must first make an *assessment* (Ricœur, 2000, p. 127). Judgement thus bears a hierarchical quality: it is the expression of a preference, an evaluation or, in Ricœur's terms, an 'approbation' (2000, p. 127). It is the construction (and articulation) of a truth *and* a subscription to it, since to judge is not just to opine and assess but also 'to take a stand' (2000, p. 128). By taking a stand – in other words, by making a decision within a space of uncertainty and in the face of contestation – the advocate asserts a particular interpretation of events, arguing that their construction of meaning in the case is better, more probable, more plausible and more acceptable than another (2000, p. 113). Just as form follows function, the advocate's argument follows from their interpretation. How they have understood the case, how they impute relevance to this or that element, where they attribute responsibility and to whom, and what they believe all of this means for the conflict at hand influences the stance they will take in public defence of their interpretation.

An analogous dialectic of interpretation and argumentation is also expressed on the plane of translation, where the uncertainty at the root of the conflict is over the 'facts' of the text-for-translation and their meaning – that is, *how* the text should be translated. When the law is silent and does not speak for itself, we call on someone to make it speak – to interpret its meaning for us, in the context of a conflict. The text-for-translation is also silent since, by definition, a text that is to be translated has been written by someone *other* than the translator, in another time and place and in another language. The translator's task is to translate its meanings into a new text, a second text, to be written in a different time and place and in a different language. Consider that texts do not speak; people do. If the text is silent, then its meanings are uncertain and their significance is yet to be determined. It requires a reader (in this case the translator) *to make it speak* – that is, to judge what it is about, to interpret its significance, in a new language and for the benefit of a new audience in a new time and place, and to defend this conceptualization in what is given in the translation. Since the text is not a truth *res ipsa loquitur*, it is a mystery to be unravelled, a possibility *to be interpreted*. Different translators will translate different texts in different ways. The translator knows that the text can always be translated differently. The case for a different way of conceiving of the text must be mounted and an argument must be made for how its meanings have been understood. For this reason, Ricœur writes that:

> [t]o show that an interpretation is more probable in the light of what we know is something other than showing that a conclusion is true. [. . .] It is an argumentative discipline comparable to juridical procedures used in legal interpretation, a logic of uncertainty and of qualitative probability. (1976, p. 78)

Participating in this 'argumentative discipline' means bringing an end to uncertainty by making a decision with regard to the text and its meanings. As with the trial, the translator makes this stand in the face of opposition, advocating through the translation their interpretation of events in the text-for-translation. In the most relevant sense, then, the translation *is* the argument. It is to the argumentative discipline of translation and the judicial interpretive acts of advocacy in which the translator engages that this chapter is addressed.

Doubt and/in translation

At the opening of a trial, Ricœur writes, we do not yet know the facts of the case, nor do we fully understand the conflict that is at its heart (2000, p. 109). The purpose of the trial is to establish the facts of the case and their significance for all concerned (2000, p. 109). A 'non-violent verbal battle' (2000, p. 109) ensues in which the different parties to the conflict set out their arguments and the judge issues a ruling. At the opening of the trial, we might say, everything is uncertain; by the end of the trial, a verdict is pronounced and with it the uncertainty is ended (2000, p. 109). The most immediate effect of this speech act 'is to decide a conflict – that is, to put an end to uncertainty [. . .]' (2000, p. x). As a form of written discourse, translation is also a speech act pronounced by a translator. 'Uncertainty' results primarily from the translator's reading of the text-for-translation, from the so-called 'source' text on which the translation is based. This uncertainty underlies questions such as 'What does this or that element mean?' or 'Why does this or that character behave in this or that way?' and it feeds anxieties as to the sociocultural, linguistic, historical and geographical locatedness of the source text and what an audience speaking a new language in a new time and place will make of it. Uncertainty in translation is grounded in the notion of *doubt* and it is at its most acute in what we might refer to as the *yes, but* factor – 'Yes, but doesn't it also mean something else?' – which is really another way of asking, 'Couldn't it be translated differently?' Here, as in the trial, where 'every judgement calls for a *but* beyond itself' (Ricœur, 2000, p. 128, emphasis mine), it is the very *existence* of doubt – and with it the invisible presence of contrary (and potentially valid) points of view – that creates a foundation for conflict, since every translation also contains within it *the possibility of its own equal and opposite.*

It is the principle of uncertainty in translation that confirms the judicial interpretive character of the translator's task because, while all texts have meaning, this meaning is only meaning*ful* in the context of a reader interpreting their meaning in the *here and now of reading*. In other words, texts do not mean things independently or transcendentally. They mean only in the space of convergence when, in Ricœur's terms, 'the world of the reader and the world of the text merge into one another' (2003, p. 378). But – that word again – in this space of uncertainty, the distance between the two worlds is not swallowed in the reading; the two sides, and the gap between them, remain. The gap itself is only bridged.

I want you to imagine a text. It can be written in any period and its author can be living or dead. Let us agree, however, that this text is going to be translated. Before the translation can be written, the translator must first read the text and establish both what it 'means' and how its meanings can be translated meaning*fully* for its new audience. We must bear in mind in this imagined textual scenario that the author's relationship to the text (and the text's relationship to its reader) is not analogous to that of a speaker and an interlocutor. In spoken discourse, the addressee of a speaker's speech – the second person *you* – is determined in advance by a properly dialogical situation in which the meaning of the speech and the meaning of the speaker are one and the same. Our text, by contrast, is not a case of spoken discourse; here, discourse has been *inscribed* and in the passage from spoken discourse to written inscription we no longer have a speaking subject – an author – who is co-present with the addressee – the reader. To the extent that the addressee of a written text is unknown, and its readership potentially limitless (Ricœur, 1976, p. 31), there is no immediacy of interlocution, only a text, detached from its author.

This detachment has profound consequences for the translator. The question 'What does the text mean?' is now complicated by the fact that the verbal meaning of the text and the mental meaning of its author are not the same. This 'semantic autonomy' (Ricœur, 1976, p. 29) means that the author's intention and the meaning of the text cease to coincide because the text is no longer the voice of someone present as a speaker is present in a dialogue:

> **Inscription becomes synonymous with the semantic autonomy of the text, which results from the disconnection of the mental intention of the author from the verbal meaning of the text, of what the author meant and what the text means. The text's career escapes the finite horizon lived by its author. What the text means now matters more than what the author meant when [they] wrote it.** (Ricœur, 1976, pp. 29–30)

This does not mean, however, that the text can mean anything, or that the text itself is authorless. Ricœur is careful to remind us that the dissolution of the intentional fallacy should not be replaced by the fallacy of the absolute text. It is still a discourse 'told by somebody, said by someone to someone else about something' (1976, p. 30). It is a human-made object, not a natural element. The authorial meaning is the counterpart of the verbal meaning and they must both be understood in terms of one another (1976, p. 30). The problem for the translator, however, lies in the fact that '[i]f the objective meaning is something other than the subjective intention of the author, it may be construed in various ways' (1976, p. 76). It is up to the reader, therefore, to take an active stance with regard to what the text offers. Like the orchestral conductor 'who obeys the instructions of the notation' (1976, p. 75), the text becomes a musical score that gives rise to a performance. These 'instructions' are not of the author *strictu sensu* but the text, and the orchestral performance that obtains from 'obeying' the musical score *is not the same as* the musical score itself. Understanding the meaning of the text is not about merely repeating the event of the author's writing of the text but generating an all-new performance event, that of appropriating the text, and its meanings, in the here and now of reading. 'In other words,' Ricœur writes, 'we have to guess the meaning of the text because the author's intention is beyond our reach' (1976, p. 75).

The guess character of translation

We are not accustomed to conceiving of translations as 'guesses'. We most often think of translations as standing for, or in place of, the texts they translate, such that the two texts – the author's text and the translator's text – become conflated in the phenomenon of the translation. It is for this reason that the dust jackets of so many works of translated literature do not bear the translator's name because the translation and the text it translates are thought to be one and the same. For all intents and purposes, we assume, the translation *is* the text. Yet the clue is in the copula of the verb *to be* – 'this (translation) *is* (the same as) the text' – which embraces simultaneously both that which the translation is *like* and *that which it is not* (Ricœur, 2003, p. 6). As with the principle of uncertainty in the drama of the trial, the judicial interpretive character of the translator's task is further confirmed through the possibility of equal and opposite conceptualizations of the text-for-translation. The *translation as copula* is both (a version of) the text and it is not. It is a text in its own right and it is a text that owes its existence to the text that comes before it. It both speaks for the text-for-translation and it speaks for itself. It is neither fully original nor is it fully derivative. It is *something else besides*.

We can conceive of this *something else besides* as a form of 'guess' because returning to the situation of the author cannot resolve for the reader what the text means in the here and now of reading. It behoves the translator to partake in an altogether different effort to make meaning of the text. As Ricœur explains:

> The text as a whole and as a singular whole may be compared to an object, which may be viewed from several sides, but never from all sides at once. Therefore the reconstruction of the whole has a perspectival aspect similar to that of a perceived object. It is always possible to relate the same sentence in different ways to this or that other sentence considered as the cornerstone of the text. A specific kind of onesidedness grounds the guess character of interpretation. (1976, pp. 77–8)

'Interpretation', here, is about taking a view – *parti pris* – on the meanings the text offers. As with the trial, the 'facts' of the text are unknown; its meanings have yet to be determined, and it is up to the translator to establish beyond all reasonable doubt that the conceptualization of the text they advance in the translation is the most appropriate, on the balance of probabilities.

Let us now place our imagined textual scenario within a concrete context of translation practice. The text is a Spanish-language comic play by nineteenth-century Cuban-Spanish Romantic writer Gertrudis Gómez de Avellaneda (known popularly today as La Avellaneda), *El millonario y la maleta* (Gómez de Avellaneda 1870/1981), which I am translating as *The Millionaire and the Portmanteau*. Written in 1870, but never performed during the author's lifetime, the play is a witty comedy set in a small town outside Madrid in the mid-1800s and tells the tale of the long-suffering widow doña Policarpa, a formidable woman of a certain age, high sensibilities and modest means. Policarpa is possessed of a singular desire: to see her three daughters wed as soon as possible, and preferably to the most eligible bachelor. When news breaks of the impending return of former resident and millionaire magnate don Esteban Cañizares, Policarpa contrives to lodge him at her home, in the hope of securing him a wife among her three daughters (any daughter will do). The whole town turns out to welcome the wealthy businessman and secure his financial backing for their many schemes – everyone, it appears, wants a piece of the man – and while an expensive case of mistaken identity indeed leads to a marriage, it is not quite the match Policarpa imagined. As part of my wider effort to translate the complete dramatic works of La Avellaneda, what might the judicial interpretive character of the translator's task look like in the case of *The Millionaire and the Portmanteau*? I want to recall my opening argument regarding uncertainty, conflict, meaning and interpretation and their relationship to the notion of translational *judgement* (Figure 1).

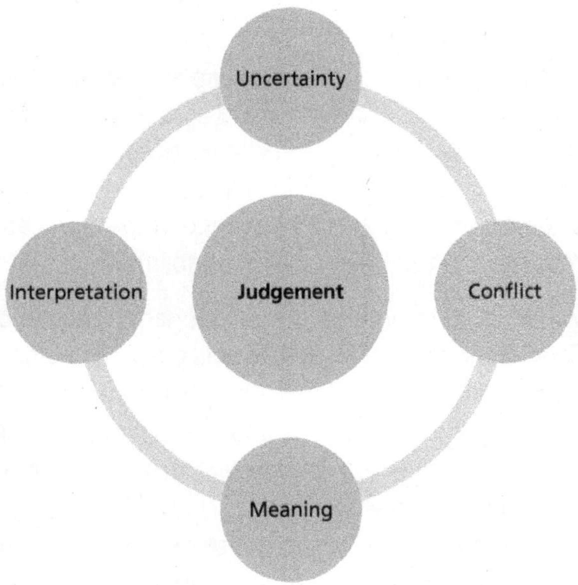

Figure 1. Constituent dimensions of the judicial interpretive task of the translator.

The principle of uncertainty surrounds the meaning of the facts of the case, which must be imputed and defended by the advocating parties to the conflict. Since meaning does not speak for itself, it must be judged. Judgement in this context is the verbal expression of a preference (argumentation), when faced with a range of possible options, for one conceptualization (interpretation) of the facts of the case over another (Figure 2).

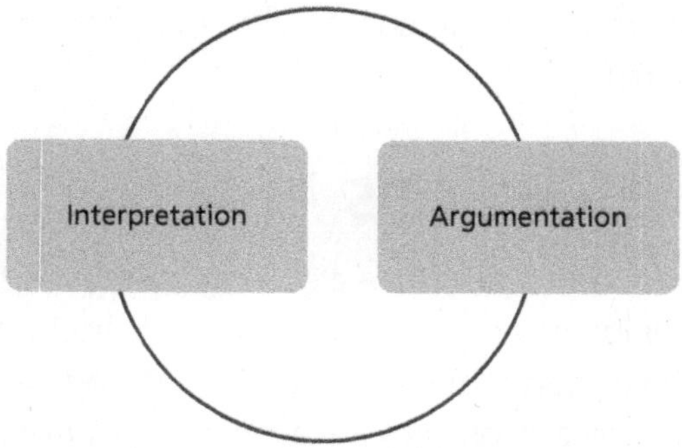

Figure 2. Dialectic of interpretation and argumentation informing the judicial interpretive task of the translator.

By staking a claim as to how the facts of the case have been understood within this space of uncertainty (and in the face of contestation), the advocate argues that their construction of meaning in the case is better, more probable, more plausible and more acceptable than another.

If we agree that from the moment of publication, and with the passage of time, a text such as Gertrudis Gómez de Avellaneda's *El millonario y la maleta* becomes autonomous with respect to its author's intentions, then the task of translation is to consider not what the author 'meant' at the time of writing in 1870 but what the play might mean to the reader in the monological silence of the here and now of reading in the twenty-first century. In short, it is not about *retrieving* meaning, in other words, but *making* it. In a complementary fashion, the task of interpretation for Ricœur 'is to reconstruct the internal dynamic of the text, and to restore to the work its ability to project itself outside itself in the representation of a world that I could inhabit' (2008, p. 18). Whereas mutual understanding in the domain of spoken discourse relies on a speaker and an addressee sharing the same time and space, no such dialogism is shared between the text and the reader, since the reader must speak in the author's place. Since the meaning of the author and the meaning of the text no longer coincide, the reader must make present what is absent, perceiving a world 'in which I could project my own most possibilities' (2008, p. 34). In the case of *El millonario y la maleta*, the reading *I* is the translator and to 'inhabit' the play is to construct (rather than retrieve) meaning within it.

The translator's GPS

At this point, I want to introduce a guiding metaphor, that of the satellite navigation device, or *sat nav*. On a smartphone, the sat nav is provided as part of the default mapping application. In many cars, sat nav screens are installed somewhere along the dashboard. The user enters the address of where they want to go and the system provides turn-by-turn voice or visual instructions that the user can follow until they reach their destination. The user comes with the questions and the sat nav gives the answers. What is interesting about sat nav technology, and it is here that we circle back to the judicial interpretive task of the translator, is that, in order to get a user where they are going, the sat nav also needs to know exactly where the user has been, since rather than showing the user *how to get to* a particular place, what the sat nav *actually* shows is the user's current position in space and time *relative* to the position they would rather be. It is for this reason that sat navs are described most accurately as global navigation satellite systems.

One of the most common global navigation satellite systems is the Global Positioning System (GPS) which is owned by the United States government. When a user operates a GPS receiver, the device establishes a connection with satellites orbiting the Earth. Wherever you are on the planet, and provided there is an unobstructed line of sight, four or more GPS satellites will be 'visible' to the device at any one time. Each of these satellites transmits information about its current position. The user's GPS device receives these signals and calculates the distance between the device itself and the satellites, based on how long it took for the signal to arrive. It uses this information to pinpoint the user's location on the Earth, relative to the satellites, and it uses this to calculate where the user is geographically, and how far away the user is temporally, with respect to the desired destination. What this means is that, despite the *ostensible* objective – to lead us to a given geographical location at some future moment in time and space – GPS devices in fact require us to locate *ourselves* in the here and now.

In the mythology of ancient Greece, we might have turned to the god Hermes for similar guidance. As the god of fertility, thieves, travellers and lies, Hermes wears many hats (the epitome of double jobbing). Often depicted as handsome, with feathered sandals which he fashioned himself, a golden staff for herding cattle, and a cap with the ability to render its wearer invisible, he was the son of Zeus and known for his athleticism. As the fastest of the gods, it was Hermes's job to ferry messages between Olympus and the people of Earth by crossing the boundary separating the two. His role was imperative – to translate divine mysteries beyond the capacity of human words into terms that mere mortals could understand. Without such a messenger, the two realms would remain forever at a distance, mutually mysterious and mutually incomprehensible. The first task of hermeneutics, the philosophical method which takes its name from Hermes, is concerned with bridging gaps in understanding – with interpreting the mysterious and making it accessible. As a hermeneutic project, translation also involves interpreting a mystery, in my case a series of mid-nineteenth-century plays written in Spanish, and making it meaningful to English-speaking audiences today. In a hermeneutic sense, the first task of La Avellaneda's translator is to facilitate understanding between the language of the source text and the language of the translation's audience. But since meaning cannot be transported wholesale from one context to another, there is something else that the translator does. La Avellaneda's plays, as with every play, every text, are a product of their time, a product of their place in the world at one particular moment. They are representative of a community of thought and reflective of a particular set of assumptions and beliefs.

What does it mean, then, to geolocate oneself as an English-speaking translator in the twenty-first century, in London, where I live, in Belfast, where I am from, relative to a text-for-translation

– *El millonario y la maleta* – written by La Avellaneda in Spanish in 1870? What impact does the positionality of the translator within their unique moment in time and space have on the nature of the translation that is produced? These questions, framed by my example of the GPS device, are strongly suggestive of the hermeneutic project at the heart of translation practice, for all translations, as with all acts of cartography, start with a mystery, a question to be answered, an uncertainty to be filled. In my case, it is La Avellaneda's dramatic works on the English-speaking stage that bear the quality of uncertainty. While she is best known for her prose, her theatrical works do not form part of the dramatic repertoire and are not generally known to English-speaking audiences or critics. Indeed, as Rauch observes, if her theatrical works have received little critical attention, 'then her comedies have been nearly [completely] ignored by scholars' (2003, p. 155). To 'inhabit' the world projected by *El millonario y la maleta* is to construct its meanings from the present place of the translator, geolocated in the here and now of reading with respect to the 'elsewhere and the elsewhen' (Johnston, 2009, p. 65) of the written inscription that is the text. It is an act of inhabitation that is filtered through the translator's own realm of experience, for as the translator I can no more come to the text *without* pre-existing knowledge through which to frame the subjective experience of the reading present (Jauss, 1982, pp. 145–6) than I can travel back in time to ask La Avellaneda what she meant when she wrote it. From this perspective, all I have is the text and the text does not speak. As the reader, I must make it speak to me.

In Act I Scene iv*, doña Policarpa, desperate to marry off her daughters Mónica, Rosa and Gabriela, announces that a potential suitor – don Esteban Cañizares – will soon arrive:

POLICARPA: (Con gravedad cómica.) Escuchad. Aquí viene también Gabriela. —¡Escuchad (Entra Gabriela) todas, hijas de Policarpa! ¡Escuchad las palabras de Policarpa, vuestra Madre!

*All excerpts from the play are presented with my own translations underneath.

GABRIELA: ¡Jesús, qué tono!

ROSA: Todas escuchamos.

POLICARPA: ¡Un millonario! ¡Un coloso de fortuna! ¡Un non plus ultra de riqueza puede ser vuestro esposo!

POLICARPA: (With comic sobriety.) Listen up, everyone. Ah, here comes Gabriela, too. —Listen up (Gabriela enters) everyone, come girls! Heed the words of Policarpa, your mother!

GABRIELA: Jesus, what a screech!

ROSA: We're listening.

POLICARPA: A millionaire! A colossus of a fortune! A non plus ultra of riches could be your husband!

I cannot help but hear the voice of Alison Steadman's Mrs Bennet in the BBC1 television adaptation (*Pride and Prejudice*, 1995) of Jane Austen's 1813 novel, exclaiming Mr Bingley's fortune of four or five thousand a year, or the flicker of excitement that circulates among the society party guests when they hear of Mr Darcy's ten thousand a year. I also cannot help reading the reaction of Policarpa's daughters through the prism of the Bennet sisters:

ROSA: (Mirándose al espejo.) Si el millonario es hombre de gusto, me parece…

MÓNICA: Si no se compactan en el cacumen las nebulosas preocupaciones con las densas de la insipiencia, para desviar las rectitudes del juicio de las infalibilidades del acierto…

GABRIELA: Por mi parte renuncio al millonario y a todos los maridos posibles. (Act I, scene iv)

ROSA: (Looking at herself in the mirror.) If this millionaire is a man of good taste, then I'll think about it…

MÓNICA: So long as the nebulous clouds of day-to-day preoccupation do not clash in his cranium with the dense fog of insipience, and rectitude of mind strays not from the infallibilities of knowledge…

GABRIELA: Well, for my part, I renounce this millionaire and all other potential husbands entirely. (Act I, scene iv)

My inhabitation of the play in this scene is that, as with the stark contrast between each of the four Bennet sisters, the different reactions of Policarpa's daughters – Rosa's vanity, Mónica's pomposity and Gabriela's apparent lack of interest in the topic of marriage – create the foundation for the comic events that ensue. But, as the translator, I remain at a distance from the play and my response results from a particular way of reading – a hermeneutic strategy. Faced with this distance, the only elements in my control are my own imputations, my investment in the text as the site of the clues I need to understand it.

A dialectic of understanding and explanation

I want to return us to the notion of advocacy in translation, by way of a legal maxim: hard cases make bad law. It is only the especially hard cases that reach the judiciary. Other, 'less difficult dilemmas' tend to be tackled through diversionary instruments or by consensus between the actors involved (Brazier, 1997, p. 341). In hard cases, legislators are often called upon to weigh in on the debate and to respond to demands for a change in the law. The legal maxim *hard cases make bad law* raises the possibility that more law is not always the right answer and that legislating hastily in the wake of a difficult case can lead to unintended consequences. A hard case is '[w]hen none of the legal dispositions drawn from existing laws seems to constitute the norm under which the affair in question might be placed' (Ricœur, 2000, p. 111), when, in other words, the questions posed do not have their answer in the law and it is left to the judge's discretion to decide under what rules the case should be placed (2000, p. 122). Discretion, Ricœur argues, is the reply to the silence of the law (2000, p. 112). We find our translational correlate when, faced with the silence of the text, the translator must apply discretion to decide what the text means *to them*. In the context of a hard legal case, judgment takes place after a deliberation – it implies a serious and careful reflection that culminates in the issuing of a ruling (2000, p. 129). Judgment, in this sense, is the terminal phase of the deliberative course (2000, p. 129). If translation is also a necessary reply to the silence of the text, and if the translator, too, issues a ruling following the deliberative passage from reflection to judgement – in the translation – then what we might describe as the 'legal effect' of what is written in the translation is not just to put an end to uncertainty by attempting to resolve a conflict through deliberative process. It is also the rendering of a decision as to how the text has been understood and *a making public* of this decision in the only place where such a decision-making process *can* be inscribed: the translation.

It is Ricœur's argument that 'the interweaving' of interpretation and argumentation on the juridical plane is symmetrical to a dialectic of understanding and explanation on the plane of the text (2000, p. 125). Understanding is a private matter, a matter for the individual, whereas explanation is a public matter. Understanding is about an individual's comprehension vis-à-vis the text, a subjective synthesis of the text's potential for meaning, while explanation is about *explication*, of articulating this range of meaning *to another*. As Ricœur argues: 'We explain something to someone else in order that [they] can understand. And what [they have] understood, [they] can in turn explain to a third party' (1976, p. 72). The essence of advocacy, in a similar vein, is to explain to others how we have understood the status quo and, perhaps, how we propose to change it in the hope that they will join us in our understanding. Viewed from this perspective, the translation that is produced by the translator becomes an act of advocacy aimed at a public – the audience of the translation – and it results from how the translator has understood the text in the privacy of reading. In the passage from private to public, and from understanding to explanation, the translator ceases to be a reader and becomes a *writer* (Figure 3).

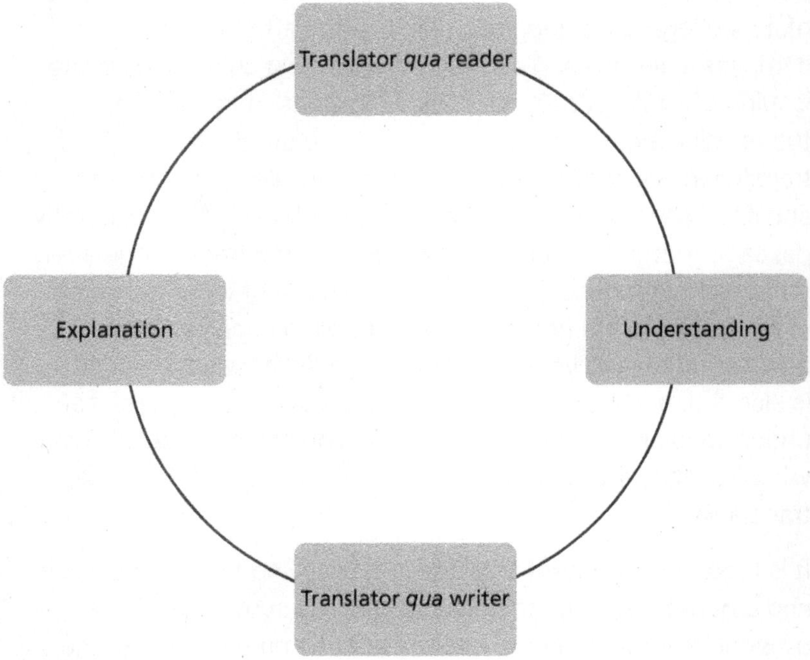

Figure 3. Circular process of reading and writing inherent in the act of translation.

That which has been understood in the text is now explained in the writing of the translation, and this translation produces a second reader – the translation's audience – instantiating an all-new dialectical engagement between a reader and a text. What is 'explained' in the translation, meanwhile, is the 'truth' of neither the text nor the author but the outcome of a deliberation that has been applied to what the text offers to the translator, or, in Ricœur's terms:

> Understanding has less than ever to do with the author and [their] situation. It seeks to grasp the world-propositions opened up by the reference of the text. To

understand a text is to follow its movement from sense to reference: from what it says, to what it talks about. (Ricoeur, 1976, pp. 87–8)

The text is static; it remains in a state of suspended animation until such time as a willing reader takes up the challenges that it offers. Actualized thus, the text is rendered contemporaneous to the translator as its present reader. As such, understanding is not so much a mode of knowledge as a mode of *being* (Ricœur, 1976, p. 4). The translation that results from this process is not concerned with resolving what things 'mean' in the text *per se* – knowledge – only what these things mean *to the translator* as the text's reader – being. The question 'What does the text say?', in this sense, gives way to the possibility of a much more interesting enquiry: 'What does the *reader* say?' If the private matter of understanding is revealing not of the author, or really of the text, but of the translator's *being*, and if the public matter of explanation is directed at a third party with the express aim that they, too, might understand, what layers of complexity can we now add to our study of advocacy in translation?

Understanding *into* the text

As in the juridical sphere, translational advocacy concerns the representation of something that is absent, of a phenomenon that does not speak, and yet which, nevertheless, must be spoken *for* – not the author but the text. As a form of explanation that follows a translator's understanding of the text, the translation becomes a form of public argument – in support of one way of seeing and being *among others*. We tend to think of translation as service provision; we want a particular text to be understood in a given second language, so we engage a translator to initiate the transfer. But in many cases, particularly in the literary and theatrical fields, translation has a declared interest. It can be about creating or building an audience for a particular playwright, or it can be about shining a spotlight on a particular topic or set of issues enshrined within a given play.

In the case of my project, my aim is to build an audience for Gertrudis Gómez de Avellaneda, a celebrated Romantic writer regarded as one of the greatest of her generation but refused a place in the Real Academia Española de la Lengua. Born in 1814 in Puerto Príncipe, Cuba, she is perhaps best known for her first published novel, *Sab* (1841), 'the only feminist-abolitionist novel published by a woman in 19th century Spain or its slaveholding colony Cuba' (Davies, 2001, p. 1). She was considered both unconventional and brilliant, at a time when it was difficult for a woman to be either of those things. By creating an opportunity for English-language readers and English-language theatre spectators to engage with the work of this writer, my broader aim is to make a contribution towards enhanced female representation in translation, on stage and in print. Given that the literary market is comprised of so few translations, and that of these even fewer are authored and translated by women, enshrined within my aims are both a status quo that my project seeks to oppose and an alternative reality for which it seeks to advocate. To locate *both* within la Avellaneda's corpus of plays is, on my part, an act of hermeneutic trust. It is my statement of belief that within the corpus an answer can be constructed to the questions that I myself pose. The corpus itself will remain unchanged, but *how* it has been operationalized in the service of my agenda will say much about the belief system that drives my enquiry.

Consider the effect this has on the non-active verb *to understand*. If, as Ricœur contends, '[i]t is always possible to argue for or against an interpretation, to confront interpretations, to arbitrate between them and to seek agreement, even if this agreement remains beyond our immediate reach' (1976, pp. 78–9), then any claim to knowledge we may associate with a translation must be reduced, since in translation, as in life, not all readings are equal. The 'private matter' of the translator's individual engagement with the text is rendered in the translation as a public ruling – but only in the sense that the guess character of translation requires the translator to judge certain elements in the text as more important than others (1976, p. 77). To make meaning out of what has been understood is itself a commentary on the object of understanding, such that the non-active verb *to understand* transforms into an active prepositional verb – to understand *into* – that identifies more transparently both the translating subject doing the understanding – the translator – and the object of their understanding – the text. Ricœur argues that, 'if it is true that there is always more than one way of construing a text, it is not true that all interpretations are equal. The text presents a limited field of possible constructions' (1976, p. 79). This places a particular responsibility on the shoulders of the translator, for not only must the translator be prepared to defend their reading of the text, but the translation itself – which is the product of their reading – must also be defen*sible*. As Ricœur reminds, judging is deciding (2000, p. 127); it means bringing an end to uncertainty through reasoned *decision*. If the translation is the translator's issuance of a ruling vis-à-vis their understanding into the drama of the text, this means that the translation must do the job of speaking for itself. The translation must be its own closing argument, the space where all internal debate between the translator and the text is closed and, as with the verdict that brings an end to the trial, the moment where conjecture must cease.

'Asked and answered' is an evidentiary objection in United States law designed to prevent opposing counsel from unduly influencing juries by asking the same question multiple times or from using their witness interrogations as opportunities for rhetorical grandstanding. Yet when faced with Gertrudis Gómez de Avellaneda's *El millonario y la maleta* as my text-for-translation, my text-to-be-understood, I must do precisely this. I must identify questions about the text and I must produce a translation that provides an answer – my answer – to the questions I myself ask (Jauss, 1982, p. 146). The main comic conceit in the play is a case of mistaken identity. In the opening scene, we learn of the imminent return of former resident and titular millionaire don Esteban Cañizares. We also realize that, despite Gabriela's declaration that she has no interest in taking a husband, this is in fact because she is in love with Emilio, whom she has encountered in Madrid six months previously when she travelled there with Policarpa's friend and neighbour doña Cayetana. Now, just as Policarpa and Cayetana make their final preparations in advance of don Esteban's arrival, they are informed by don Crisanto that he has already seen don Esteban descending from his carriage. How can he be sure it is don Esteban and not someone else? they ask. Crisanto replies that it can be no other for the man was well dressed and the vehicle carried a portmanteau bearing the initials *E* and *C*:

CAYETANA: E. C.?

POLICARPA: Esteban Cañizares.

CRISANTO: ¡Claro! La dicha maleta no tardó en ser reclamada por su dueño, lo mismo que un cajón marcado con iguales letras. (Act I, scene vii)

CAYETANA: E. C.?

POLICARPA: Esteban Cañizares.

CRISANTO: Of course! The portmanteau in question was soon collected by its owner, as well as a crate bearing the same letters. (Act I, scene vii)

The audience soon realizes that the 'E. C.' in question is not Esteban Cañizares but the lovestruck Emilio Coello, who has also resolved to visit the town – in search of Gabriela. It is from this point onwards that every person encountered by the young Emilio mistakes him for don Esteban Cañizares.

One of the most potentially significant of these encounters from a translation perspective involves a brief episode of code switching between Spanish and the Basque language Euskara. The misapprehension in this encounter is on the part of Vélez, who describes himself to Emilio as the son of don Fulgencio Vélez the chemist, who married the cousin of don Esteban Cañizares's mother's sister-in-law. Since everyone wants Emilio – that is, don Esteban Cañizares – to give them money or favour, Vélez is no different and explains that his sister has recently given birth and wants don Esteban to have the honour of lifting the child out of the baptismal font as its godfather. As they take their leave of each other at the end of this exchange, Vélez tells Emilio that the child is the very image of him. This is no surprise, Vélez adds, since every family has their own distinctive 'look', to which Emilio replies:

EMILIO: ¡Cierto! El aire de familia es cosa que no se despinta nunca. —Vaya V. con Dios, amado primo.

VELEZ: Nada de cumplimientos. *Agur*. (¡Qué amable y qué rumboso!). (Act I, scene xix, emphasis mine)

EMILIO: Absolutely! The family look never fades. —God speed, good Sir, beloved cousin.

VELEZ: No need to stand on ceremonies. So long. (How kind and generous he is!). (Act I, scene xix)

For this reader, the use of *agur* – a common form of communicating 'goodbye' in the Basque Country today – raises many questions. The Spanish and Portuguese surname Vélez is thought to be of German origin and has been associated with the Basque Country. Would it have been obvious to Emilio, and to a contemporary audience, that the character of Vélez was from the Basque Country and therefore the presence of Euskara in an otherwise Spanish-language play fully expected? What does it add to the character of Vélez to have him say goodbye in this way? It is worth considering, for example, whether the use of *agur* might have lent the character a congenial or familiar air if Euskara is his preferred language of communication, or to what extent any implicit sociocultural assumptions surrounding the use of the term might need to be made explicit. Should I translate the *agur* into English along with the rest of the Spanish, even if this means losing the linguistic distinctiveness that characterizes the original speech? How important to the exchange is the *agur* term *per se* versus the *effect* on the reader to which its presence gives rise? The translation I have provided here opts not for a contrast between languages – Spanish and Euskara, English and something else – but for a change in register – from 'God speed' to 'So long'. I am still at the understanding stage with this one. The reader will have to wait for the published translation before I can hope to explain the decisions I have made.

Conclusion

'All understanding,' writes George Steiner, 'and the demonstrative statement of understanding which is translation, starts with an act of trust' (1998, p. 312). In translation, this statement is about refusing objectivism because translators cannot claim to forget themselves in the acts of reading that precede the writing of their translations. I cannot unread Austen's *Pride and Prejudice*, I cannot stop being Northern Irish, I cannot stop being someone who lives in London, and all those other aspects of my identity, knowledge, experience and beliefs that will influence my reading of both the world around me and the texts I translate. I cannot put my subjectivity to one side and translate neutrally because there is no such thing as detached interpretation. And yet this circular dialectic is also about refusing absolute knowledge; it is about recognizing my subjectivity while also attempting to remain open minded, to be *aware* of the extent to which the horizon through which I experience the world influences what I read into the plays I translate. It is about recognizing that the distance between me and the time and place in which the text was written originally means that I cannot capture its world of meanings within the singular vision a translation provides. These meanings are not essences contained within the text, waiting for me to acquire them. They are dramatic possibilities that I will seek out as part of my translational enquiry into the drama of the text. As with the results of all research, the translation represents my interpretations, my imputations, that I signal in the here and now of writing and which I craft deliberately, judiciously, to speak to my audience both in a language they can understand and in such a way that my message is made real. Constructing, rather than retrieving meaning, translation is an interpretive act that creates its own object and, like the GPS device that cannot lead its user to a destination without first distinguishing the user's point of departure, translation geolocates the translator within the time and space of reading and writing, as an advocate for one reading among many. To write, to research, to translate is to start from an investment of belief in the object of study, to advocate for a reading of the text and to argue for this explanation in the writing of the translation. The selectiveness of this complex engagement with a text makes translation as judicious a process of meaning making as any other.

References

Brazier, M. (1997) Hard cases make bad law? *Journal of Medical Ethics*, 23 (6), 341–3.

Davies, C. (2001) Introduction, in Davies, C. (ed), *Sab: By Gertrudis Gómez de Avellaneda*. Manchester: Manchester University Press, pp. 1–28.

Gómez de Avellaneda, G. (1841) *Sab*. Madrid: Imprenta de la calle del Barco.

Gómez de Avellaneda, G. (1870/1981) *El millonario y la maleta*, in Castro y Calvo, J. M. (ed), *Biblioteca de autores españoles desde la formación del lenguaje hasta nuestros días (Continuación): Obras de doña Gertrudis Gómez de Avellaneda IV*. Madrid: Ediciones Atlas

Instituto Europa de los Pueblos (2019) 'Agur'. Una poderosa palabra del euskera, que tiene una gran historia. 14 July. Available from: http://institutoeuropadelospueblos.org/2019/07/14/agur-una-poderosa-palabra-del-euskera-que-tiene-una-gran-historia/ (Accessed: 1 March 2023).

Pride and Prejudice (1995) BBC1, 24 September–29 October.

Ricœur, P. (1976) *Interpretation Theory: Discourse and the surplus of meaning*. Trans. D. Pellauer. Fort Worth, TX: Texas Christian University Press.

— (2000) *The Just*. Trans. D. Pellauer. Chicago and London: University of Chicago Press.

— (2003) *The Rule of Metaphor*. Trans. R. Czerny with K. McLaughlin and J. Costello. London: Routledge.

— (2008) *From Text to Action*. Trans. K. Blamey and J. B. Thompson. London: Continuum.

Jauss, H. R. (1982). *Toward an Aesthetic of Reception*. Trans. T. Bahti. Minneapolis, MN: University of Minnesota Press.

Johnston, D. (2009) Historical theatre: The task of the translator. *TRANS: Revista de Traductología*, 13, 57–70. DOI: 10.24310/TRANS.2009.v0i13.3155.

Maitland, S. (2017) *What is Cultural Translation?* London: Bloomsbury Academic.

Rauch, K. (2003) The 'quid pro quo' of Gómez de Avellaneda's 'El millonario y la maleta'. *Romance Notes*, 44 (2), 155–61.

Saínz, E. (2014) Introducción: Un acercamiento a Gertrudis Gómez de Avellaneda, in Saínz, E. (ed), *Gertrudis Gómez de Avellaneda: Obra selecta*. Madrid: Editorial Verbum, pp. 9–17.

Steiner, G. (1998) *After Babel: Aspects of language and translation*. Oxford: Oxford University Press.

2

Between: An example of collaborative, advocating theatre-making by spoken language interpreters

Beverley Costa and Teresa Murjas

Overview

Between is a play written collaboratively by members of UK-based performance company Around the Well. It was created through an interdisciplinary development process, shaped and facilitated by Dr Beverley Costa and Professor Teresa Murjas. The stories told in the play are rooted in real experiences and have been fictionalized and/or edited for purposes of both dramatization and anonymization. The play's purpose is to advocate for increased understanding of interpreters' experiences and for improvements in their working practices and conditions. The play was originally performed in the UK, in contexts where English was a shared language. The readers were members of Around the Well, a group of interpreters, and during the performance they first identified as themselves before going on to voice the words of others.

The play is written for six multilingual readers (R1, R2, R3, R4, R5, R6) and should be delivered directly to the audience, always acknowledging their presence. The languages mentioned in the script below are those that were used by the readers for the play's first performances, many of whom are professional interpreters. A further key aspect of these early performances was their staging as collaborative readings; the presence of a script, held and referred to throughout by each reader, was of central importance.

Between: an example of collaborative, advocative theatre-making by spoken language interpreters

According to the 2021 UK census, for 880,000 people in the UK who cannot speak English well, and for 161,000 people who cannot speak English at all, spoken language interpreters are crucial. Yet in the world of health and social care, people's multilingual identities, multilingual experiences and multilingual lives continue to lack visibility and acknowledgement. While some health and care practitioners may welcome an interpreter as a partner in the helping relationship, many practitioners regard them as an inconvenience to be tolerated or disregarded (Gryesten *et al.*, 2023). For spoken language interpreters, the emotional labour of professionally navigating such environments can take its toll.

In 2017, six people came together to raise the profile of these issues in a way they hoped could generate progressive action. Their lived professional experiences within the contexts outlined above, their shared interest in collaborative theatre-making and their profound curiosity about the advocative potential of live performance together led them to form a theatre company, which they named Around the Well. The company is based in the Department of Film, Theatre and Television at the University of Reading and its founder members are Dr Teresa Murjas, Professor in Theatre and Performance, and Dr Beverley Costa, a psychotherapist and CEO for 18 years of Mothertongue, a Reading-based multi-ethnic counselling and interpreting service. Beverley now runs the Pásalo Project, which builds on Mothertongue's legacy through creative knowledge sharing. The professional spoken language interpreters with whom we co-created *Between*, the company's first performance, are Kamaljit Dosanjh (Punjabi and Urdu), San Maya Gurung (Nepali), Joanna Mungai (Polish) and Guida Shields (Portuguese). All six company members contributed material to and performed *Between*, which received its inaugural staging in a programme funded by the European Commission at Europe House in London on 15 March 2019. The play was also performed by the company at Birkbeck, University of London, the Open University, Milton Keynes, and the Spring School of the UNESCO Chair Refugee Integration through Languages and the Arts, University of Glasgow. Around the Well received a grant to perform *Between* at King's College, London, as part of the *Language Acts and Worldmaking* Fair in 2019. Extracts from the play were also performed by the company as part of an online event at the University of Southampton.

Between is a play devised through a collaborative method progressively developed by Costa and Murjas, which enabled us to cofacilitate Around the Well's discussions, improvisations, creative explorations, drafting, editing and, ultimately, rehearsals. Our method evolved through consistent interdisciplinary dialogue enriched through reflection on varied, intersecting critical approaches and performance models, including applied, community, multilingual, verbatim, autobiographical, therapeutic, didactic and activist. The version of *Between* published here should be regarded as a working script, captured at a particular moment of its evolution, following several public performances (both live and live-streamed) and a further retrospective editing stage.

The company's interdisciplinary, collaborative approach is variously evident throughout this published play text in its episodic, multi-vocal form; its self-reflexivity; its emphasis on storytelling, direct address and ethically shaped/presented verbatim testimony; its interest in the performativity of translation processes; its strategic playfulness; its didactically inflected strands drawing on

Mothertongue's wealth of therapeutic experience and interpreter training, including the organization's two National Lottery-funded anthologies of interpreters' stories: *In Other Words* (2015) and *In More Words* (2017). All these dimensions of *Between* express the need for ensemble performance. Notably, the play's initial and closing stage directions emphasize the presence of the playscript, to be synchronously opened, held, used throughout by each ensemble member, then synchronously closed again at the end. This underlines the collective act of reading, of being 'on book', that *Between* represents, alongside its aim to retain a partially unpolished, 'raw' and speculative approach to storytelling. Indeed, we have experimented with the idea of describing *Between* as a collaborative performance-lecture or lecture-performance.

The fact that all company members have experience of migration, either personally or as part of their immediate family background, manifests directly through the play's thematic content. In narrating experiences of displacement, identity and interpretation, *Between* shares examples of positive transformations that people have experienced through migration and multilingualism. It also investigates experiences of exclusion – when some people understand and some people do not understand what is being said – bringing to life broader ongoing cultural and political debates about insider and outsider status, within the UK, Europe and beyond.

As already noted, the materials embraced by *Between* have been drawn from a range of sources and stem from experiences that are both personal and professional. Whereas the play's introductory episodes personalize its themes through exploring everyday situations rooted in, for example, its creators' family lives, their ultimate purpose is to frame and contextualize the professional experiences that will be described, depicted and probed in later episodes. These relate specifically to health and social care and the role that spoken word interpreters play in this context. The majority of the play's scenes illustrate – from the perspectives of interpreters, practitioners and clients – the challenges and ethical dilemmas of interpreting for people who are in sensitive situations. As the play notes, its purpose is not to share 'excellent practice' but to speak advocatively, together, of embodied, lived experiences. It is wonderful to us how the publication of our playscript in this volume amplifies the voices in *Between*.

The play's title meaningfully signals our intention to engage the public in reflection on the position of the spoken language interpreter. People who are in the position of interpreting spoken languages often report being perceived as marginal transmitters or ultimately expendable mediators, yet their role can be crucial for communication, whether they are working in, for example, a medical or social services context, a legal context or a conflict zone. Spoken language interpreters often work with the most vulnerable people in society. They hear and render distressing messages. Interpreters frequently report that their personal lives can be negatively affected by the impact of listening to and rendering stories of torture, violence and human trafficking (Geiling *et al.*, 2022). Rendering those highly emotional messages in the first person (as interpreters are frequently asked to do) tends to exacerbate the detrimental impact, something the play also seeks to communicate through its self-reflexive approach to conventions of role and audience address.

Between is now situated within a larger project by Around the Well, called UTTER. This aims to raise awareness of the processes and impacts of spoken language interpreting. Despite many studies and guidelines, interpreter-mediated care is still often inadequate (Ogunnaike *et al.*, 2022).[1] UTTER seeks to change practice in interpreter-mediated health and social care by engaging with the urgency of the situation. For example, the performance-lecture form of *Between* enables the urgent and compelling stories and experiences in interpreter-mediated care today to be heard, received and acted on with empathy and immediacy. Besides raising awareness, UTTER develops training programmes which have an impact. Training in working

[1] For example, the British Psychological Society guidelines for psychologists working with interpreters or the Royal College of Speech and Language Therapists checklist for working with interpreters.

effectively with interpreters has begun to be delivered by a variety of providers.[2] Appropriate training for practitioners to work with interpreters is vital and it is urgent, as this comment from one participant on a training course illustrates:

> **A lot of today's content gives us stronger arguments to make a case with the organizations we work with, where we see poor practice, and at best a lack of nuance in their approach. I think the organization I work for hasn't really got to grips with what it means to live in a diverse society, and diversity of language is obviously a really important part of that.**

UTTER attempts to convey all three perspectives of the interpreter-mediated communication triad – client/patient, care practitioner and interpreter. Whereas *Between* particularly, though not exclusively, highlights interpreters' perspectives, our upcoming creative intervention, which has been seed-funded by the University of Reading, will begin with the release of a short film that considers what is at stake for primary care physicians right here, right now, in interpreter-mediated encounters. We look forward to the launch of the film in spring 2024 on the following platform: https://www.pasaloproject.org/resources.html.

Between: A multilingual play

Devised by Beverley Costa and Teresa Murjas, with Kamaljit Dosanjh, San Maya Gurung, Joanna Mungai and Guida Shields. Edited by Teresa Murjas.

Scene 1

(Six readers stand next to each other, in a semi-circle, facing the audience. They share one common item of costume: white shirts. They all hold the playscript and open it together to signal the opening of the performance.)

[2] The Pásalo Project alone delivered training to 939 practitioners in statutory and voluntary sector mental health, speech and language therapy and refugee support organizations between 2021 and 2022.

Reader 1: Between.

All Readers: Between.

Reader 2: Stories told from in-between places.

Reader 3: *(R3 translates 'Stories told from in-between places' into another language. In the original performance, this was Polish.)*

Reader 2: *(R2 translates R3's words into English.)* Stories told from among different places.

Reader 1: *(R1 translates R2's words into another language. In the original performance, this was Spanish.)*

Reader 2: *(R2 translates R1's words into English.)* The stories which are told, and which arise from the different places.

Reader 4: *(R4 translates R2's words into another language. In the original performance, this was Nepali.)*

Reader 2: *(R2 translates R4's words into English.)* Stories that come from different places.

Reader 5: *(R5 translates R2's words into another language. In the original performance, this was Punjabi.)*

Reader 2: *(R2 translates R5's words into English.)* Stories that come from different, different places.

Reader 6: *(R6 translates R2's words into another language. In the original performance, this was Portuguese.)*

Reader 2: *(R2 translates R6's words into English.)* Stories which come from different, different places.

ALL: Stories told from in-between places.

Scene 2

Reader 3: *(Greets the audience in Polish and says their name.)* Born and educated in Poland. I never planned to leave my country, but my journey has lasted nearly 20 years.

Reader 5: *(Greets the audience in Punjabi and says their name.)* Born in an Indian Punjabi village. When I was 14, my family travelled to England. We settled in Leicester, where I continued my education.

Reader 3: I wasn't forced to leave Poland. I needed new opportunities, to improve my family's life and education. We lived in Finland and Canada before arriving here.

Reader 5: I learned three languages at school, Punjabi, Hindi and English. But maths and science were my forte. After a degree in Medical Laboratory Sciences, I worked in a hospital path lab.

Reader 3: My journey's been filled with adventure. New languages, cultures, lifestyles! And I keep on learning. Communication. Not always easy. Determination. That's what it takes, to harness so much change . . .

Reader 5: My husband's job took us to various countries. I learned to communicate with local people. This made me think hard. About migration. Then, when I settled in Reading, I wanted to work with migrant communities.

Reader 3: I looked for a job. I was a trained psychologist, but the profession differs in every country. Then, I received an email. *Mothertongue* is running a workshop, it said. On interpreting in mental health environments.

Reader 4: *(Greets the audience in Nepali and states their name.)* Since 2010 I've worked for Reading Borough Council. As a Nepali interpreter.

Reader 3: I read the email again. My experience seemed relevant. I attended the workshop. I've never looked back. What started out as volunteering is now my full-time job and I love it! I'm an interpreter! Helping others to communicate, helping to explain . . .

Reader 6: *(Greets the audience in Portuguese and states their name.)* Born and raised in Portugal. At 25, I married and moved to the UK.

Reader 5: I was complaining to my father-in-law, 'Main kush karna chuhndi haan, jad Anjali school hundi aa.'

ALL: *(In English.)* 'I want to do something while Anjali's at school.'

Reader 5: *(In English.)* I WANT TO DO SOMETHING WHILE ANJALI'S AT SCHOOL. How about this, he said, brandishing a leaflet. The Annual General Meeting. Of *Mothertongue*. There, I listened to the CEO's speech. Her sincerity and passion inspired me. Patients suffering from poor mental health need clear information. So do their caregivers. I knew this from family experience. I also knew I had a lot to offer.

Reader 4: My husband served in the British Armed Forces for 18 years. He fought in two conflicts. In November 2006, while visiting our daughter, we decided. We want to settle in the UK. Sixteen months after submitting our application, the Home Office informs my husband you have no physical ties to the UK. Your application has been rejected. Our appeal takes a further 14 months.

Reader 6: From a very young age I felt this huge affinity with the English language. And culture. I'd always wanted to be here. Now, I was living the dream.

Reader 4: Then, we meet a Gurkha campaigner. We start campaigning for our right to settle. Some British former soldiers set up a charity, The Forgotten

Gurkhas. I volunteer to complete forms and act as a mediator between Gurkha veterans and our British supporters. And so, you see. We're still here!

Reader 6: Then the children started to arrive. And I began to think about roots. How important they are. Choosing names was really interesting. It went on and on, sometimes for days. Each child received an English and a Portuguese first name. Plus, my last name. And my husband's.

Reader 4: In 2013 I first made contact with *Mothertongue* and met the CEO. I'm still part of this interpreting family, I feel this so strongly. As interpreters, we're bound by rules of confidentiality. We cannot share these experiences with anyone else. But *Mothertongue* was a professional, confidential space. After a challenging session, we could empty our hearts.

Reader 2: Hello! My name is (*shares name*). I'm a bilingual theatre maker. My parents were Czesław and Irena.

Reader 6: At my second son's passing-out parade, this led to a funny situation. We arrived and were asked for his name, to which we replied . . .

ALL: Peter Brown.

Reader 6: Not on the list, they said. I looked across and spotted a veeeeery long line. Pointing to it, I grinned and said, I think it could be this one . . .

Reader 2: Peter.

Reader 3: Filipe.

Reader 1: da Silva.

Reader 4: Carvalho.

Reader 5: Brown.

Reader 6: That's the one!

Reader 1: *(Greets the audience in Spanish and states their name.)* My mum's family came from Russia and Poland. My mum was Jewish. Her name was Rosa.

Reader 6: I've been like a bridge. For my children. Between two very different cultures. Now they know how to enjoy both. They are bilingual and Portugal is their home, as much as the UK. Watching them interact with my Portuguese family fills me with joy.

Reader 2: Murhas. That's how most people read my surname. Are you Spanish, they say. No, is the answer, though I can see the logic. Actually, there's a village called Murjas in Ardèche and Drôme, in France. Perhaps that's my ancestral home. There is some archival evidence . . .

Reader 1: Rosa taught me a bit of Yiddish. I like to try out Yiddish phrases. But we pronounce words differently. We say *baigel* when everyone else says...

ALL: *Baygel!*

Reader 1: . . . and we say *schlap* when everyone else says. . .

ALL: *Schlep!*

Reader 2: My parents were from Poland. They came here after the war. They were born in neighbouring villages but met in Derby, of all places, and fell in love. Apparently, my father proposed on a bridge. That's where I was born. Not on a bridge, I mean, in Derby. I grew up speaking a mixture of Polish and English at home. We didn't call a lorry a *ciężarówka*, like authentic Polish people. We called it a *lora*.

Reader 1: I could have learned more Yiddish. A lot of my family spoke it and Rosa was fluent. But I didn't learn more Yiddish because my family were always *broigus* with each other . . .

ALL: *Broigus?*

Reader 1: Another Yiddish word. The meaning of *broigus* is a feud. It involved people not talking to each other. For years.

ALL: *(React with shock and regret.)*

Reader 1: And my father? I never learned his language either. What a shame, a waste, a loss.

Reader 2: During the week I attended a comprehensive school. On Saturdays, it was time for Polish school. Apparently, this was better for my immortal soul than watching daytime TV. Who needs *Charlie's Angels* anyway! Since then, I've had three books published. They're English translations of Polish plays. Mainly by Gabriela Zapolska, who died in 1921. She's buried in Lviv, formerly known as Lwów. Two of her plays combine Yiddish and Polish.

Reader 1: No surprise then that many years later, after training as a psychotherapist, I set up an organization called *Mothertongue*. It was a counselling service, multi-ethnic, culturally and linguistically sensitive. It was through *Mothertongue*, in Reading, that I met all my fellow performers here this evening.

Reader 2: Joshua Fishman was a linguist. He specialized in the sociology of language and bilingual education.

Reader 1: The revitalization of minority languages.

Reader 2: Born in Philadelphia, USA in 1926 . . .

Reader 1: Yiddish was one of the languages of his childhood.

Reader 2:	Every day at the dinner table, Joshua's father would ask him and his sister . . .
Reader 1:	*(In Yiddish.)* 'And what have you done for Yiddish today?'
Reader 2:	*(In English.)* 'And what have you done for Yiddish today?'
ALL:	*(To the audience.)* 'And what will you do for Yiddish today?'
Reader 1:	This is what Joshua Fishman had to say about language: 'A shared language is a gift, a marker of identity, and a specific responsibility to future generations.'

Scene 3

(Reader 1 takes a photograph from their pocket and looks at it. The group gather around them to look at the photograph.)

Reader 6:	She has a photograph with her father and one of her sons.
Reader 5:	A young woman and older man sit next to each other.
Reader 4:	She wears two necklaces, her baby son held in her lap.
Reader 2:	The baby wears a pair of stripey shorts.
Reader 3:	The man is smiling broadly.
Reader 6:	The man and the baby hold hands.
Reader 3:	And the young woman is kissing the man on his forehead.
Reader 1:	A good translator must be both a sage and a fool, Isaac Bashevis Singer once wrote, and where do you find such a strange combination?

Scene 4

(The readers return to their original places, in the semi-circle facing the audience.)

Reader 1: The title of this story is *Eleftheria*, which means Freedom. Costas Charalambous Pouyiorous was born on 29 January 1919. He would have been 104 years old this year. Costas was born in a village north of Famagusta, in Cyprus. It was a small village by the sea. Costas's father was the headmaster of the only school for all the children in this village. But he was removed from his job by the British government in the early 1930s because he was active in the fight for independence from British rule. At that time, Cyprus was a British colony. When he was arrested by the British government, he signed his name not as Pouyiorous but as *Eleftheria*, which means Freedom.

Reader 3: Costas's father was a strict disciplinarian with his own children . . .

Reader 2: . . . but Costas's mother had a very generous spirit. She never let anyone who came to the door begging for food go away hungry.

Reader 3: Costas took after his mother . . .

Reader 2: . . . and even to this day, in Cyprus, people remember him as a kind-hearted young man.

Reader 1: At the age of 17, in 1936, he decided to try his luck and travel to the UK. To London, where he had heard the streets were . . .

ALL: PAVED WITH GOLD.

Reader 1: Times were hard for the Pouyiorous family after the arrest of Costas's father. Although Costas supported the struggle for independence, he was also very pragmatic. He applied for his . . .

ALL:	BRITISH PASSPORT.
Reader 1:	He bought a ticket for his journey on a ship that would take him as far as Southampton. It was lucky that Costas decided to make this journey in 1936 and not the following year. In 1937, the regulations changed . . .
Reader 3:	. . . as regulations do . . .
Reader 1:	These changes meant that . . .
ALL:	BRITISH PASSPORTS . . .
Reader 1:	. . . were only issued to people from Cyprus who could speak English . . .
Reader 2:	. . . (he could not) . . .
Reader 1:	. . . and to people who had enough money to pay a bond of 30 pounds.
ALL:	HE DID NOT.
Reader 1:	He spent one of his first Christmases in the UK billeted with a family in Norfolk.
Reader 2:	'He is staying with us for the New Year and he can't understand why . . .'
Reader 3:	'. . . shortly before midnight on New Year's Eve . . .'
Reader 2:	'. . . we push him out of the house . . .'
Reader 3:	'. . .give him a piece of coal . . .'
Reader 2:	'. . .and tell him to come straight back in again . . .'
Reader 1:	The explanation?
Readers 2 and 3:	'He is the darkest man we know.'
Reader 1:	Not till several years later did someone explain to him the tradition of . . .

ALL: FIRST FOOTING.

Reader 1: Now you may or may not be wondering how Costas ended up in Norfolk. His destination had been London. Remember? You may already have taken note of the date when his journey began.

Reader 2: 19 . . .

Reader 3: 30 . . .

Readers 2 and 3: Six.

Reader 1: Not long after his arrival in the UK, war was declared. Costas had a . . .

ALL: BRITISH PASSPORT . . .

Reader 1: . . . and THAT meant he was a . . .

ALL: BRITISH CITIZEN . . .

Reader 1: . . . and THAT meant he was eligible for conscription into the . . .

ALL: BRITISH ARMY . . .

Reader 1: . . . to be precise, the Royal Artillery, 56th London Division, also known as . . .

ALL: **THE BLACK CATS!**

(All Readers fall into line, military fashion.)

Reader 1: And so, he found himself on an army parade ground in Norfolk, turning left . . .

(All Readers turn to their right.)

Reader 1: . . . when he should have been turning right . . .

(All Readers turn to their left.)

. . . and wondering why people kept shouting at him. Being on army training, he discovered, was an excellent motivator for learning a language.

Reader 3: Costas Charalambous Pouyiorous lived, worked and raised a family in the UK for 55 years, until his death in 1991.

Reader 1: I am one of his daughters.

(All Readers turn to face the audience.)

Reader 4: She told me her mum and dad's journeys have shaped her and she has shaped their stories.

Reader 5: She mentioned that as a child immersed in three different cultures, languages and religions, she got to know about misunderstanding and breaking down, about connecting and building back up.

Reader 1: That experience led me to pass on family stories to my own children, so they can begin new chapters. When *Mothertongue* came to an end, I set up an organization called *Pásalo*.

Reader 6: *Pásalo* means . . . pass it on!

Reader 5: That's what she wants to do with the knowledge and experience we've gained.

Reader 1: And that's what we're doing here, tonight.

Scene 5

(Reader 6 steps forward, closer to the audience, the rest cluster together at some distance behind them.)

Reader 6: Está-se a tentar dizer uma coisa.

Reader 2: You are telling something.

Reader 6: Revolta-se com tudo.

Reader 1: You revolt at everything.

Reader 6: Tem-se problemas.

Reader 3: You have problems.

Reader 6: Quere-se dizê-los ao médico.

Reader 3: You want to tell them to the doctor.

Reader 6: Sabe-se Português.

(There is a pause. The group behind Reader 6 seem touched by these words. Reader 6 waits patiently, with hope and expectancy, looking out towards the audience. Eventually Reader 6 speaks again, very gently, having sensed the group's response. This time, Reader 6 inflects their words as a question, quietly confident that someone will translate).

Reader 6: Sabe-se Português...?

(Reader 4 decides to speak out, with equal gentleness, translating both the words and their new intonation).

Reader 4: You know Portuguese...?

(Pause. Reader 6 needs the intonation to be correct and so patiently and more firmly underlines their original way of saying the sentence)

Reader 6: Sabe-se Português.

(Reader 4 responds accordingly by translating the intonation correctly and firmly).

Reader 4: You know Portuguese.

Reader 6: Não se consegue dizê-los em Inglês.

(Pause.)

Reader 4: You can't tell them in English.

(Pause. Reader 6 further strengthens the tone of their communication).

Reader 6: Não se consegue dizê-los em Inglês.
Isso é a primeira coisa . . . penetra como uma seta.

Reader 4: You can't tell them in English . . .

Reader 5: . . . that's number one . . . already enters you like an arrow.

(Pause. Everyone acknowledges internally the significance of these words. A renewed sense of collective purpose now moves

the readers into the next section of the scene, which should flow collaboratively, calmly, and directly. The group increasingly supports Reader 6 in conveying what needs to be conveyed).

Reader 6: Em segundo lugar . . . a segunda pessoa . . . essa pessoa sabe a sua língua.

Reader 1: Secondly . . . a second person . . . that person knows your language.

Reader 6: Ela pretence à sua cultura.

Reader 1: She is someone from your own culture . . .

Reader 6: Isso é como se pensa.

Reader 1: That is how you think.

Reader 6: Fala-se daquilo por que se passou.

Reader 5: You talk about what you have lived through.

(Pause.)

Reader 5: You talk about what you have lived through . . .

(Pause.)

Reader 5: You talk about what you have lived through . . . ?

(Pause.)

Reader 6: Fala-se daquilo por que se passou. Questionando-se sobre o que ela estará a pensar.

Reader 4: You talk about what you have lived through. Wondering what she is thinking.

Reader 6: Isso penetra como uma segunda seta.

Reader 2: That enters you as the second arrow.

(Pause.)

Reader 6: Isso penetra como uma segunda seta.

Reader 4: It makes you upset.

(Pause.)

Reader 5: Of course, it makes you upset.

Reader 6: Isso deixa-nos tristes, claro que nos deixa tristes.

(Readers move back into their semi-circle facing the audience.)

Scene 6

Reader 1: Have you ever heard this saying?

Reader 6: The original is unfaithful to the translation.

Reader 2: The title of this story is . . .

Reader 3: Nie wiem o co chodzi . . .

Reader 6: OR . . .

Reader 2: I don't know what's going on.

(Reader 2 steps forward and stands on a small stool; the others move in closer to them, looking up.)

Reader 1: In 1941, after Operation Barbarossa, her maternal grandfather was released from forced labour in Siberia. Bolek chose to join the Polish Armed Forces in the West. He saw action in Italy and the Middle East.

Reader 2: A photograph from that time shows him standing next to a bicycle, his soldier's beret set at a jaunty angle.

Reader 3: After the war, Bolek settled in England. At first, he lived in a Displaced Persons camp near Market Harborough. Then he moved to Derby with his young family, who had survived the war in a refugee camp in Zambia.

Reader 4: In Poland, Bolek had been a master blacksmith. In the Midlands, his physical strength came in handy on building sites and railways.

Reader 2: Bolek rarely asked me for anything. But one summer's day when I was about ten years old, he sat me down in his front room and told me in Polish that he needed to buy a . . .

Reader 3: . . . skórzany pas do golenia.

Reader 2: . . . Oh, I . . .

Reader 3: SKÓRZANY PAS DO GOLENIA.

Reader 2: Well, I didn't know what a . . .

Reader 3: Skórzany pas do golenia . . .

Reader 2: . . . was. SO, he explained.

Reader 4: A wide leather belt with a hook at either end. Needed to sharpen his cut-throat razor.

Reader 3: Skórzany pas do golenia, no!

Reader 2: Bolek continued in Polish . . .

Reader 3: I went to the barber's shop recently. Down the road. To see if I could buy this thing. But I couldn't make myself understood. The barber shook his head, at least twice, and shrugged his shoulders . . .

Reader 5: And Bolek ran out of words.

Reader 3: What do you call it in English?

Reader 5: Said Bolek.

Reader 2: I'm not sure, I said, but I think it translates as . . .

ALL: SHAVING BELT.

Reader 2: . . . Shaving belt?

(Pause.)

Reader 3: Are you sure?

Reader 2: He asked.

Reader 3: Because I've tried describing it to the barber, but he seems not to understand?

Reader 2: No, I am not sure . . .

Reader 5: . . . she said . . .

Reader 2: But there's a slim chance I could be right.

Reader 3: So, will you go the barber's . . .

Reader 5: . . . said Bolek . . .

Reader 3: . . . and ask him for one. I will give you the money. I will walk you to the shop and wait for you close by.

Reader 6: She thought about it in silence. Who knows what held her back?

Reader 2: I felt a wave of embarrassment flooding my body.

Reader 4: She had to come up with a compromise.

Reader 2: I can write it down for you on a piece of paper . . .

Reader 4: . . . she said . . .

Reader 2: . . . and then you can go and tell the barber what you want.

Reader 3: Dobrze . . .

Reader 6: That means 'all right' . . .

Reader 4: . . . said Bolek sternly . . .

Reader 3: Here is a pencil and here a slip of paper. Write it down for me and that is what I will do.

(The pace quickens.)

Reader 2: He exits to the kitchen. What's best to do? I muse. I know! Let me clearly spell out the English words 'shaving belt' phonetically, using the Polish alphabet, in capital letters, on the paper, and then Dziadek can take that piece of paper with him to the barber's and read out the words. Then he will have what he needs. And I will have done something good.

Reader 5: I mean there was no doubt this was both a sophisticated and a foolproof plan.

Reader 2: I picked up the pencil and traced the letters carefully . . .

S-Z-E-J-W-Y-N-G-E

B-E-Ł-T

(A large placard magically appears bearing these letters, held up by Reader 6.)

Reader 2: I used the letter 'L' with a line through it because that represents a 'W' sound in Polish. I knew that, with his accent, Bolek would naturally pronounce the word BELT as BEWT and so reasoned that this approach would make it easier for him to communicate. In Polish the letter 'W' represents a 'V' sound. So, there it was, on the slip of notepaper, marked out clearly by my ten-year-old hand: SZEJWYNGE BEŁT.

I went into the kitchen and presented it nervously to my grandfather.

(Reader 6 coyly approaches Reader 3 with the placard and curtsies shyly.)

He folded it neatly and tucked it into his jacket pocket.

(Reader 3 gruffly takes the placard and moves to the back of the space, where they stand still holding it aloft. Everyone is delighted with themselves, but then gradually begin to exchange looks and look at their watches and whisper to each other. Reader 2 looks increasingly uncomfortable standing on the stool.)

Reader 6: A couple of weeks went by and things were silent on the grandparent front. They didn't have a phone, so she couldn't call. She was sure it had all gone swimmingly.

(Reader 1 puts on a blue headscarf, tying it under their chin.)

Reader 2: But one day *Babcia*, or Grandma, Weronika, came round to our house, her blue headscarf knotted tightly under her chin and her mouth set in a sharp line.

Reader 1: Don't shoot the messenger . . .

Reader 2: . . . she said . . .

Reader 5: . . . or words to that effect . . .

Reader 1: . . . but why did you give your grandfather a piece of paper with some bad spelling on it?

Reader 2: ... I blushed deeply.

ALL: SHAME ON YOU!

Reader 2: What do you mean, *Babcia*? I gave the notepaper to Dziadzio so that he could read out the name of the thing to the barber and get what he needed.

Reader 1: Well, that's not what he thought . . .

Reader 6: . . . said Weronika.

Reader 1: He thought you'd written it out so that he could SHOW it to the barber and get what he needed. So, first he passed the barber the slip of paper, since he was too embarrassed to speak. He did even try to pronounce the words you'd written, but the barber only smiled, shrugged his shoulders and shook his bald head. Your grandfather thinks you have done this on purpose.

ALL: SHAME ON YOU!

Reader 2: I was torn between laughter and tears. How I wished I'd gone to the barber's with Dziadek. The two of us together, an unshakeable alliance! I pictured myself addressing the barber in a clear English accent.

Reader 1: My good man, we need to buy a shaving belt!

Reader 3: *(Passionately, brandishing the placard.)* SKÓRZANY PAS DO GOLENIA!

ALL: *(Whispering to the audience.)* A shaving belt . . .

Reader 2: Then maybe, just maybe, the barber would have understood.

Reader 6: For this, her first serious commission as an interpreter, she had balanced on a razor's edge.

(Reader 2 steps down from the stool and all props and costumes are put away.)

Scene 7

(Reader 4 takes out their mobile phone and starts doing some searches.)

Reader 4: Hey, listen, I searched the word 'interpreter' on Google yesterday. It came up as *do bhashe*. That's quite similar to Hindi, right?

Reader 5: Yes, *do bhashyia*, it means 'bi-lingual'.

Reader 4: Is there a word for 'interpreter' in Punjabi?

Reader 5: Nope, there isn't.

Reader 6: In Portuguese it's *intérprete*. But often, people address me as '*é a minha translator*'. The official word for translator is *traduttora*. People tend to use the English word – 'translator' – though, but that's still not an 'interpreter', is it?

Readers 4 and 5: No, absolutely not, etc. . . .

Reader 1: When I train practitioners, they're often really surprised to learn that the correct term for somebody who translates the spoken word is an 'interpreter'. They don't really like it because they want somebody who will transfer the meaning accurately between two languages. The word 'interpreter' makes them think that somebody will be giving their own opinion and perspective.

Reader 2: The following stories turn our attention to the role of the professional interpreter.

Reader 1: We are always mindful of confidentiality and professional boundaries. We faced our own dilemma when deciding to use our work as the starting point for storytelling.

Reader 5: This isn't about sharing excellent practice. The stories are all drawn from real experiences.

Reader 6: However, we have anonymized and fictionalized where necessary. No one is identifiable.

Scene 8

Reader 6: *(Scene title in Portuguese.)*

Reader 5: *(Scene title in Punjabi.)*

Reader 3: *(Scene title in Polish.)*

Reader 4: *(Scene title in Nepali.)*

Reader 2: The title is 'Don't Shoot the Messenger'.

Reader 5: This story is about interpreting at a child protection meeting. Ten people are there. Professionals and members of the child's family, including his mother. They are making a crucial decision about whether the three-year-old boy can return home to his mother or should remain in care. Everyone's voice can only be heard and understood through the interpreter.

Reader 6: In the story, I sit next to the mother for whom I am interpreting.

As I sat next to her, I could see her hands clenching, then unclenching, nails bitten to the quick. I could sense her anxiety. If I could only soften the delivery of what was being said. But everything that's said must be interpreted.

How many times had I heard that, how many times repeated it?

Knowing the right way doesn't make it any easier.

Words alone are easy to interpret, but what's hidden behind them is so very hard to convey. I'm like the only football spectator who can see both sides of the field.

I watch both teams playing their game and only I am in a position to understand both sides. Each side relies on me, but all I'm translating are the words. There's so much more, unseen by them, that I must hold inside.

I look at the boy's mother. As if sensing what's coming, the colour drains from her face. A new stillness pervades her body. Her hands lie in her lap. She no longer wishes to please or resist us.

All that was said came from other mouths, but it was from mine she heard it. The words I uttered did not miss their mark. And I had pulled the trigger.

Scene 9

(Three chairs are arranged in a triangular formation in the space, each facing the audience.)

Reader 1: This scene explores the perspectives of the client, the interpreter and the practitioner.

(Reader 1 approaches the chair from stage right.)

Reader 1: I am playing the practitioner.

(Reader 5 approaches the chair from stage left.)

Reader 5: I am playing the interpreter.

(Reader 2 approaches the chair between the others.)

Reader 2: I am playing the client.

(The three readers take their seats. The practitioner tries to look at the client. The client and the interpreter look at each other throughout the whole conversation. Long pause as they enact this.)

Practitioner to Client:	Thank you for coming in today, I need to ask you a few questions.
Interpreter to Client:	Thank you for coming in today, I need to ask you a few questions.
Client to Interpreter:	Is this going to take long? I need to collect my son from school.
Interpreter to Practitioner:	Is this going to take long? I need to collect my son from school.
Practitioner to Client:	No, don't worry. There are only a few questions. We should be finished in 15 minutes.
Interpreter to Client:	No, don't worry. There are only a few questions. We should be finished in 15 minutes.
Practitioner:	*(Tries to smile at Client, but Client is looking at Interpreter.)* Well then, let's begin. Can you tell me when you came to the UK?
Interpreter to Client:	Well then, let's begin. Can you tell me when you came to the UK?

(Pause.)

Client to Interpreter:	Four years ago. Why does she want to know that?
Interpreter to Practitioner:	Four years ago. Why does she want to know that?

(Pause.)

Practitioner to Interpreter:	*(Crossly.)* Listen, do you mind not looking at her all the time? How is she going to trust me if I can't even make eye contact?

Interpreter to Practitioner: Sorry, I'll try not to look at her any more *(pause)*. But she may wonder why I've changed my behaviour. She might be offended.

Practitioner to Interpreter: *(Crossly.)* Yes, well. Would you please just do what I ask?

(Interpreter is about to speak to Client and leans in towards them.)

Practitioner: *(To the audience.)* Typical. Who do these 'interpreters' think they are! Five minutes doing some . . . snowflake diploma . . . in 'Speaking Your Own Language' and they come over all Nobel Peace Prize. It takes years, I mean honestly, YEARS, of VERY HARD WORK, to qualify as a doctor in this country. How difficult is THAT to understand?

Interpreter: *(To the audience.)* Typical. Who do these 'doctors' think they are? Sixteen years studying a bunch of made-up ailments! Then, well, it's like they're Yoda, saving us from the Dark Side. To be an interpreter, THAT takes skill, resilience and GREAT determination. But it's beyond them!

Client: *(To the audience.)* Do you know what they're saying? Are they talking about me? This is really horrible. All I can hear is blah, blah, blah. I NEED to collect my SON from SCHOOL.
Will you please ask them how long it will take?

Scene 10

(Reader 6 takes out their diary.)

Reader 3: *(Polish translation of scene title.)*

Reader 2: 'A Day in the Life of an Interpreter.'

Reader 4: *(Nepali translation of scene title.)*

Reader 3: Five a.m.

Reader 6: Wake up!

Reader 2: Six a.m.

Reader 6: Get out of bed. Wash my hair.

Reader 4: Do you set an alarm?

Reader 6: No, I just wake up.

Reader 5: 7:40.

Reader 6: Leave the house.

Reader 1: 8:30.

Reader 6: Millman Road Health Centre, Reading. Interpreting. GP appointment.

Reader 3: Nine o'clock.

Reader 6: Eye clinic at Royal Berkshire Hospital, Reading. Interpreting. Eye appointment.

Reader 4: Ten o'clock.

Reader 6: Outpatients, two at Royal Berkshire Hospital, Reading. Interpreting. Endoscopy appointment.

Reader 1: 11:50.

Reader 6: Children's outpatients. Wycombe Hospital. Interpreting. Routine follow-up appointment.

Reader 1: One p.m.

Reader 6: Rehearsal for performance of *Between*. Working lunch.

Reader 3: Three p.m.

Reader 6: South Block. Royal Berkshire Hospital. Orthopaedic Department.

Reader 2: What was the appointment?

Reader 6: No idea.

Reader 1: Why not?

Reader 6: They only tell you where to go. No other information till you get there.

Reader 2: But, you still don't know?

Reader 6: Patient didn't turn up. I had to wait the full hour just in case.

Reader 5: Did you still get paid?

Reader 6: Yes, because it wasn't cancelled. The patient just didn't turn up. Agency policies vary. If we cancel, we have to pay them. If the agency cancels, sometimes we get paid, sometimes we don't...

Reader 1: 4:20.

Reader 6: Endoscopy Unit. Royal Berkshire Hospital. Interpreting. Colonoscopy appointment.

Reader 3: 6:00 to 6:10.

Reader 6: I sit in the car.

Reader 3: 6:10 to 7:00.

Reader 6: Drive home.

Reader 2: Seven p.m.

Reader 6: Arrive home. First stop: the bathroom.

Reader 5: Eight p.m.

Reader 6: Dinner.

Reader 1: Nine p.m.

Reader 6: Turn on computer and printer. Scan timesheet. Open agency portals. Process and upload timesheet. Prepare timesheets for tomorrow. Fall asleep on keyboard.

(Reader 6 puts their diary away.)

Scene 11

Reader 3: *(Scene title in Polish.)*

Reader 6: *(Scene title in Portuguese.)*

Reader 1: *(Scene title in Spanish.)*

Reader 4: *(Scene title in Nepali.)*

Reader 5: *(Scene title in Punjabi.)*

Reader 2: The title of the story is 'Lost for Words'.

Reader 3: It was an assessment session. With the NHS Child and Adolescent Mental Health Service. The eight-year-old boy had arrived from Poland three years ago, with his family. When he started primary school, he couldn't speak any English and struggled to make friends. He was really unhappy and hid his feelings to protect his parents. Which worked, for a while. But something had changed. Something had brought the family to this appointment. In the midst of the assessment the therapist, Lucy, said to the boy.

Reader 1: Can you tell me what happened?

Reader 3: The boy said nothing. Not a word. Suddenly, he became withdrawn, looked ashamed, stared at the ground. That's when I realized how serious it was. But I had no information about the incident, so his behaviour mystified me.

Reader 1: Would you feel better if your mum told us what happened?

Reader 3: Said Lucy to the boy.

Reader 1: If you like, you can leave the room.

Reader 3: He nodded, and Lucy led him outside. After a while, she returned and carefully closed the door. That's when the mother burst into tears. As Lucy gently persuaded her to speak, everything became clear.

Reader 2: A few days ago . . .

Reader 3: . . . she said . . .

Reader 2: . . . when I got back from work and went into his room, there he was, standing on his desk, with a rope tied around his neck.

Reader 3: This was not the answer I had expected. Empathy flooded through me. Tears welled up inside me. But still I struggled to take it in. I couldn't even remember the English word for rope. I floundered in a lost place without words. When Lucy had finished her notes, and the mother calmed down, the boy returned to the room. To me he seemed more relaxed. And shortly afterwards, the appointment ended.

The appointment has ended. I'm sitting in the car park in my silver Toyota. The midday sun is shining. It is very hot. I'm looking inside myself. I can't see anything around me. I'm thinking about my daughter who's the same age as the boy. About all her friends. About all the other children I've interpreted for. I sit for an hour in the Toyota, and I can't stop crying. Why do I carry on doing this job? Indeed, you may wonder . . .

Scene 12

Reader 1: 'An Interpreter's Guide to Job Satisfaction'.

Reader 4: For home visits, I travel by bus. I always arrive first. Ready to work. In winter, come rain or shine, you'll see me wrapped in my huge scarf, waiting opposite the house, watching every car. Is that the practitioner, I wonder, that car just parking now?

Reader 6: Sometimes people ask me, why's your car so clean? It's my mobile office! I'm always in transit. Every day – Google Maps. Where to go, where to park. All to a special soundtrack.

Reader 5: Ha! *Swan Lake*, you mean?

Reader 6: No, I mean Tchaikovsky's 1812 Overture.

Reader 3: Excellent choice.

Reader 6: Last year, I supported a long-term client through a turning point. Twenty years I've interpreted for him. There was one session – it changed his life and mine. Afterwards, I basically danced back to my car. I sat behind the wheel and turned on the radio. Brass fanfare! Cannons! Bring it on! So, I bought the CD.

Reader 4: I love that feeling. Especially when the practitioner says what a difference you've made. It happens a lot. On the way home, I stop at the library. I browse the shelves and always end up at the same spot. *Three Men in a Boat*, there's the copy, with its worn dustcover. I arrive home, take off my scarf, kick off my shoes, leave everything in an enormous heap, make a strooong cup of tea, sink into the sofa, and sail away down the River Thames.

Reader 3: Birds flying high . . .

Reader 4: You know how I feel . . .

Reader 6: Sun in the sky . . .

Reader 4: You know how I feel . . .

Reader 5: Breeze driftin' on by . . .

Reader 4: You know how I feel . . .

Reader 3: It's a new dawn . . .

Reader 6: It's a new day . . .

Reader 5: It's a new life . . .

Reader 4: For me . . .

ALL: And I'm feelin' GOOOD!

Scene 13

Reader 3: *(Scene title in Polish.)*

Reader 6: *(Scene title in Portuguese.)*

Reader 2: The title of this story is 'Ticking the Boxes'.

Reader 5: What a beautiful sunny day! It really was. I was travelling in my yellow Mini when the phone rang. It was Kim from the agency.

Reader 2: I have a last-minute appointment . . .

Reader 5: Kim said breathlessly . . .

Reader 2: It's in Slough. They need someone now! Can you get there?

Reader 5: This is a typical conversation with Kim. She encourages practitioners to give us fair warning, but honestly, it's rare. No problem, Kim, I said, playing James Bond to her Miss Moneypenny, I'm on my way. And I put my foot down.

Reader 1: This is a story about a home visit. An interpreter has been booked by a mental health practitioner to interpret for the patient's mother. The patient is a 19-year-old man. The story begins when the practitioner and interpreter enter the house.

Reader 5: As the interpreter, at the very least I expect an introduction . . .

Reader 1: But the practitioner gets straight to the point . . .

Reader 5: She addresses everyone present . . .

Reader 2: The patient's father . . .

Reader 3: And sister . . .

Reader 5: And me . . .

Reader 6: I'm here to obtain parental consent for your son. He's being kept in hospital under the Mental Health Act. His order runs out tomorrow.

Reader 5: Then she addresses the father.

Reader 6: As I said on the phone, your wife is listed as the older parent. We need to extend the order so that your son can remain in hospital. That's why I need to speak to your wife. Only the older parent can give consent.

Reader 5: I stand there in the room, watching. Still waiting, actually, for an introduction. The young man's sister speaks up . . .

Reader 3: We didn't know if you were coming. And my dad's angry about how you spoke to him on the phone.

Reader 2: My fatherly opinion is not important. Even though I do everything for this family! I can speak English and can tell you everything you need to know. But since you prefer to speak to my wife . . . well . . . she will tell you exactly the same thing. She can speak English too.

Reader 1: He storms out . . .

Reader 5: I'm wondering, if everyone can speak English, why on earth am I here?

Reader 1: The mother comes in and the practitioner asks again about consent. She replies . . .

Reader 4: My husband can speak for all family.

Reader 5: I can hear the father pacing in the hallway. My presence embarrasses him. The mother understands enough English and doesn't really need me. But the sister wants an ally to help her be heard – other healthcare providers have let them down. She speaks fluent English too.

Reader 1: So, what happens next?

Reader 5: The sister talks about the brother's illness, diagnosis and treatment. The mother lets her do the talking. And the consent, to the extent it's given, comes from the sister too.

Reader 3: My brother will only take his medicine if someone gives it to him. Unless he can get that help outside, he needs to stay in hospital.

Reader 5: As we're leaving, the practitioner apologizes to the father.

Reader 6: I'm sorry if you felt left out. But we have to follow procedure.

Reader 5: But by then, she had lost his respect.

Scene 14

Reader 2: The title of this story is 'Do Not Assume'.

Reader 1: I'm a psychologist. My client is a new mum who's been struggling with food. Through her Arabic-speaking interpreter, I ask her what she's eaten today. Hardly anything, it seems. It's Ramadan, the interpreter tells me. That's why she's fasting. I understand you're fasting because of Ramadan, I say to the client. The interpreter translates. The client falls silent and appears cross. An uncomfortable pause. Then the client says, I'm not a Muslim. And I'm not fasting. I'm dieting to lose weight. I find myself getting cross with the interpreter. Later on, I take time to reflect. I was the only person in the room who couldn't understand what was being said. I'd felt vulnerable and exposed. When the interpreter offered cultural information, I seized it, wanting to appear culturally sensitive. Now my first rule is 'Do Not Assume'. I should have first checked with the client whether the information about Ramadan was relevant to her.

Scene 15

Reader 2: Let's play 'Ethical Dilemmas'! Players: 6–120 *(depending on size of audience)*. Set-up time: one minute. Playing time: a lifetime. Random chance: it depends. Skills required: simple social skills, no bluffing. Brace yourselves!

Reader 1: Dilemma one.

Reader 5: 'The Laughing Interpreter'.

Reader 3: You're a healthcare practitioner running a surgery. One patient and one interpreter are present. Through the interpreter, you've just asked your patient a question. The patient starts to reply. Even though you don't understand the words they're saying, you can see from their body language that the patient is upset. You expect the interpreter to convey the translation of the patient's words to you. Instead, the interpreter is laughing. What do you do?

ALL: *What* do you do!!?

Reader 5: Dilemma two.

Reader 2: 'The Weeping Client'.

Reader 3: You're a psychologist. You're running an interpreter-mediated consultation with a patient. Through the interpreter, you ask the patient a question. They start to cry. You decide to leave some space for the patient to . . . continue crying. You sense the interpreter is quite uncomfortable about this. Suddenly, the interpreter offers the patient a tissue and speaks to the patient in their shared language. This isn't what you'd intended. You wanted to offer the client time to cry without interruption. What do you do?

ALL: What do *you* do!!?

Reader 5: Dilemma three.

Reader 1: 'The Lying Family'.

Reader 6: You're a hospital manager. You're walking through the hospital reception area. You overhear a conversation between a patient's relative and the receptionist. The relative asks forcefully why hospital policy has changed. Why aren't relatives allowed to interpret for their own family any more? The receptionist replies, 'The hospital's found that when relatives act as interpreters for their families, they frequently lie.' As hospital manager, what do you do?

ALL: What do you *do*!!?

Scene 16

Reader 2: The title of this story is 'Hidden Words'.

Reader 3: An interpreter accompanies a social worker to a home visit. To assess the care needs of an elderly couple. The story shows how, sometimes, addressing people in authority, and being open, can prove challenging for clients. When interpreters feel that a client is being misunderstood by a service, do they intervene or not?

Reader 5: *Namaste!* Please enter!

Reader 4: An energetic woman, Uma, invites us in. The previous year a stroke paralysed her husband and impaired his speech. The couple has moved to a two-bedroom council flat. This visit is a review to see how they're faring in their new home. Uma shows us around the flat. She seems quite friendly and cheerful. Then we sit near her husband in the lounge. The social worker asks questions and Uma's replies seem cold and distant. When asked how she's coping, Uma remarks . . .

Reader 5: If he falls down, or falls sick, I'm helpless! What can I do?

Reader 1: Call 999!

Reader 4: Replies the social worker.

Reader 5: But I don't speak English . . .

Reader 4: Uma claims . . .

Reader 1: Then call your son and he can phone an ambulance or the doctor . . .

Reader 4: . . . Advises the social worker. Uma gives me a desperate look and says . . .

Reader 5: . . . I can pick up the phone and talk to anyone, but I don't know how to dial the number. I never went to school, you know.

Reader 4: She shoots me an accusing look.

Reader 5: Anyway, in those days, there were no schools in our village.

Reader 4: She sighs deeply, then comes that look again, it seems to be saying . . .

Reader 5: You should know better.

Reader 4: Nothing feels right. Uma keeps refusing support, then saying she can't cope. Clearly, she wants something else, but what? Villagers from the hills of Nepal tend to favour indirect communication – I know this. I'm aware that Uma's gestures, her body language, they're telling us something else. But there's nothing I can do. I can't translate the unspoken. Some support is arranged and Uma clearly isn't happy. Outside, the social worker asks if there's anything I want to say. This unlocks an opportunity. I express my suspicions and we return to the flat. The social worker asks Uma directly.

Reader 1: Tell me what you really want.

Reader 4: Uma umms and ahhs, her hands fluttering. She speaks in a dialect I can't understand. Then she calls out someone's name and a young woman appears . . .

Reader 2: Mother-in-law wants her son to be allowed to live with her, in the council house, so that he can help her out . . .

Reader 4: At last Uma's actual wishes and all her excuses are fully understood.

Scene 17

Reader 1: This story explores a nurse's perspective. Diary of a Community Practice Nurse. Tuesday 27 November.

Reader 2: Dear Diary. Not a good day. Young boy, asylum seeker. Unaccompanied. Mental health assessment. Woman arrives to interpret. Smarter than usual. Black suit, crisp white shirt. Assessment starts. All seems fine. Am following standard questionnaire, as ever. Standard question: do you have any family? So, I ask him. Do you have any family? I wait, pen poised, looking down at the form while the interpreter speaks. Silence. Table starts to shake. What's going on? I raise my eyes. He's banging his head against the table. Blood everywhere. On the interpreter's white shirt. I freeze. No idea what to do. Interpreter told me later I just sat there saying, Oh my God, oh my God, what have I done? What have I done? No idea whatsoever. Me, a trained nurse. Not a clue. In English, I'd have known. In my own language. But the boy spoke his language. Kurdish. Somehow, I felt outside it. No idea what to do. Interpreter had to calm him, help him get clean. Why? She asked him. Then he looked at me. *Apparently*, he said, what does she think I am? A stone?? Of course, I come from a family.

Just because they are all dead does not mean I come from nothing. Completely devastated. No sleep. I keep on seeing the boy. I keep on seeing the boy. Everywhere! And the interpreter's shirt.

Scene 18

(Six readers stand next to each other, in a semi-circle, facing the audience.)

Reader 1: Between.

All Readers: Between.

Reader 2: Stories told from in-between places.

Reader 3: *(R3 translates 'Stories told from in-between places' in another language. In the original performance, this was Polish.)*

Reader 2: *(R2 translates R3's words into English.)* Stories told from among different places.

Reader 1: *(R1 translates R2's words into another language. In the original performance, this was Spanish.)*

Reader 2: *(R2 translates R1's words into English.)* The stories which are told, and which arise from the different places.

Reader 4: *(R4 translates R2's words into another language. In the original performance, this was Nepali.)*

Reader 2: *(R2 translates R4's words into English.)* Stories that come from different places.

Reader 5: *(R5 translates R2's words into another language. In the original performance, this was Punjabi.)*

Reader 2: *(R2 translates R5's words into English.)* Stories that come from different, different places.

Reader 6: *(R6 translates R2's words into another language. In the original performance, this was Portuguese.)*

Reader 2: *(R2 translates R6's words into English.)* Stories which come from different, different places.

ALL: Stories told from in-between places. *(The readers close their scripts. They acknowledge each other and the audience.)*

THE END

References

Geiling, A., Knaevelsrud, C., Böttche, M. and Stammel, N. (2022) Psychological distress, exhaustion, and work-related correlates among interpreters working in refugee care: Results of a nationwide online survey in Germany. *European Journal of Psychotraumatology*, 13 (1). DOI: 10.1080/20008198.2022.2046954.

Gryesten, J. R., Brodersen, K. J., Lindberg, L. G., Carlsson, J. and Poulsen, S. (2023) Interpreter-mediated psychotherapy – a qualitative analysis of the interprofessional collaboration between psychologists and interpreters. *Current Psychology*, 42. DOI: 10.1007/s12144-021-01345-y.

Mothertongue (2015) *In Other Words (The Interpreter's Story)*. London: Mothertongue. Available from: https://www.pasaloproject.org/uploads/8/7/8/7/87874356/in_other_words_final_june_2015.pdf (Accessed: 27 October 2023).

Mothertongue (2017) *In More Words: First International Anthology of Interpreters' Stories*. London: Mothertongue. Available from: https://www.pasaloproject.org/uploads/8/7/8/7/87874356/in_more_words_final_27917.pdf (Accessed: 27 October 2023).

Ogunnaike, Y., Hyde, A. and Somanadhan, S. (2022) Prevalent practices amongst healthcare professionals in paediatric settings in using medical interpreters for families with limited national language proficiency: A narrative scoping review. *International Journal of Nursing Studies Advances*, 4. DOI: 10.1016/j.ijnsa.2022.100109.

3

Advocating for translations in languages education

Katie Brown

Overview

As other chapters in this book show, translation is a field fraught with power imbalances and advocates – be they translators, publishers, agents or readers – all play a significant role in determining whether and how a text reaches a new audience. These advocates and their actions are shaped by their individual positioning and perspectives, including their cultural background. In this chapter, I argue that attention to the processes through which translations are produced and circulate can facilitate debates in the classroom about how we see ourselves and others, which are fundamental to intercultural understanding. I advocate for teaching translation literacy within language programmes and reflect on my experience of teaching a course in which students are asked to read translations and consider the role played by translators, publishers and critics in shaping the imaginaries of the Hispanic world held by English-speaking readers.

Introduction

As the introduction to this volume reminds us, advocacy comes from the Latin *advocare*, meaning 'to summon' or 'call in'.

Translations, as entry points to other cultures, do not just appear in new contexts; they are the product of advocacy, of a range of agents – including translators, publishers or reviewers – inviting elements of one culture into another. Chapters in this volume demonstrate that the way these advocates position themselves – such as the 'translator's GPS' in Sarah Maitland's terms – and the social relations between them, play a significant role in shaping what gets translated and how. Just as these advocates are geo-located, readers have their own positioning, including pre-existing ideas of the cultures from which translated texts originate. I argue, therefore, that studying the whole process of translation and reception is a way to understand how elements of one culture are 'called in' by another and thereby critically reflect on questions about identity and power dynamics.

Intercultural understanding is at the core of Languages education. The Quality Assurance Agency (QAA) subject benchmark for Languages, Cultures and Societies, which defines standards for languages teaching at UK universities, sets out:

> **The study of languages enables students to understand the similarities and differences between cultures, in the broadest sense [...], and the customs and practices of everyday life. In this sense it is inherently intercultural. The study of languages enables students to understand ideas and events that cross national boundaries, the current and historical relationships between countries, and the ways in which other countries interact with the UK. In this sense, it is transnational.** (QAA, 2019, p. 7)

This suggests a back and forth, developing a critical understanding of one's own language and culture in relation to another. In this chapter, I argue that the study of translations in a broad sense, looking at not only linguistic questions but rather the whole process of a text moving from one audience to another, can facilitate the debates about how we see ourselves and others, which are fundamental to this process of intercultural understanding.

As I will put forward in this chapter, this broad approach to translations could be conceived as an extension to the concept of 'translation literacy' (see Klitgård, 2018).

Translation literacy understood as an academic skill enables students to easily move between different languages and cultures, enhancing an intercultural and more comprehensive understanding of the world and fostering sounder research practices throughout their academic life (Antón, 2020, p. 178).

By bringing these perspectives on translation into the Languages classroom, translations become a way not only to learn more about the language and culture of study but also to turn a critical gaze on the receiving culture, to interrogate the expectations of English-speaking readers and how our own perceptions of other cultures are formed. Translator Suzanne Jill Levine writes, 'Knowing the other and how we receive or hear the other is a fundamental step towards knowing ourselves' (2009, pp. xiv–xv). This approach, I believe, fits the recent call by Naomi Wells *et al.* (2019) for Languages as a discipline to learn from Ethnography, particularly in 'allowing students to reflect more explicitly on what it means to inhabit and negotiate the border territories of languages and cultures'.

The inspiration for this chapter – and the module on which it is based – came from a thought-provoking International Translation Day, hosted by the British Library, the Free Word Centre and English PEN on 30 September 2016. The day began with a plenary session highlighting how many stages a book goes through on its journey from one language market to another. Chaired by translator Daniel Hahn, the session featured a literary scout, a publisher, a sales manager, a publicist, a bookseller and a newspaper critic. Where, I asked myself, were the educators? There are academics who recommend the works they study to publishers of translations, though the paths for doing so are limited. And, of course, academics who are also translators, who bring the texts that they study to new audiences both in the classroom and through their translations, reflecting on this process in their research. As Sophie Stevens explores in her chapter in this volume, working with students on a translation can be a valuable starting point for the critical reflection at the foundation of academic research.

More generally, educators have a role in bringing literature in translation to our students, given that among our core values is understanding people from different places and backgrounds. When I asked my final-year class if they read translations, they said no, with the exception of one student noting having read *Anna Karenina*. Although I teach Spanish, I would like my students to be curious about Croatia or Korea, to be open to new ways of seeing the world – and reading translations can help them do that. In this respect, I was particularly looking forward to the panel at that International Translation Day on 'The Current State of Translation in Higher Education' but found that it focused almost entirely on how we can better involve professional translators in university programmes in translation and improve the translation training offered at universities. I wholeheartedly agree that professional translators – like Ros Schwartz (2019), who spoke engagingly about her experiences of teaching translation in university contexts – should be hired as lecturers in translation. Their expertise and experience of translation as an industry are invaluable for training future generations of translators. But we could also make better use of them to understand the translation industry as a force in shaping the ways readers in one country view those in another, with their insights into how and why the books they translate come to be chosen for translation instead of others, or the cultural background they needed to translate that text well.

In this chapter, I will argue for the value of studying translations as part of Languages education, with a particular focus on how study of the entire process surrounding a translation – including what gets chosen for publication, how the work is translated, how it is marketed and how it is received – promotes critical reflection on intercultural communication and the formation of national imaginaries. After outlining some of the ways in which the translation and reception of texts both reflect and shape the imaginaries of one nation held by readers in another, I will reflect on my own undergraduate module, 'Hispanic Fiction in English: Translation and Reception', as an example of the embedded study of translations in Languages education. I detail my pedagogical approach and syllabus in the hope that they may be adapted in other classrooms and for other languages.

Translation, reception and imaginaries of 'Others'

Lawrence Venuti asserts, 'Translation wields enormous power in the construction of national identities for foreign cultures' (1995, p. 19). We can challenge definitions of national identity in an increasingly globalized world, and the relevance of translations when imaginaries of other countries are ever more influenced by sources including news coverage, film and television, and the internet. Nonetheless, I maintain that the limited amount of Hispanic fiction translated into English and the reception of these books continue to shape ideas about Spanish-speaking countries for English-speaking readers in ways which as yet have lacked critical attention. In a 1995 article for *Latin American Research Review*, Clifford Landers named around 20 Latin American authors likely to be known to general readers. I am sure you can guess some: Gabriel García Márquez, Jorge Luis Borges, Carlos Fuentes, Octavio Paz. Landers then states, 'This roll, however striking, is tiny when compared with the many talented and original voices that are unlikely to be heard outside of their country of origin' (1995, p. 254). The international appetite for Latin American literature has undoubtedly grown in the nearly 30 years since this article was published, thanks to initiatives such as Bogotá39 and the work of numerous independent publishers, yet the number of Latin American writers who are widely known outside of the continent remains small, to say nothing of writers from other Spanish-speaking countries such as Equatorial Guinea. What is it that leads to this handful of books being published in translation? Do they share any characteristics? Do readers then believe that these books are somehow representative of their country of origin? That these are the best books published in that language?

In their introduction to *Postcolonial Translation: Theory and Practice*, Susan Bassnett and Harish Trivedi claim, 'Translation is not an innocent, transparent activity but is highly charged with significance at every stage' (2012, p. 2). Decisions must be made not only when rewriting the source text in the target language. Why is a certain text chosen for publication in another language? Who makes this decision and what factors influence them? Who is chosen to translate this text? Will they write a preface or translator's notes? In what collection will the book be published? What will the cover design be? How will it be marketed? How will it be reviewed, by whom and in which publications? Will it win any prizes? Each step in the process of a text moving from one language market to another is 'charged with significance' because the decisions made by publishers, editors, translators, book designers, marketing managers, reviewers and prize juries have enormous power to shape what is read and how. I propose adopting here Lawrence Venuti's 'hermeneutic model of translation', which understands translation as 'an interpretive act which varies the form, meaning and effect of the source text according to the intelligibilities and interests of the translating culture' (2017, p. 8). Starting with the concept of the 'translator's interpretive force' (Venuti, 2017, p. 9), I suggest discussing the 'interpretive force' of the publisher, the cover designer, the marketing manager, the reviewer and the reader, as part of a Languages class, to consider what they tell us about the existing imaginaries or expectations of the source culture, as well as how translations as cultural artefacts shape these ideas.

This is a growing field of research within Translation Studies. Rita Wilson (2013), for example, asks key questions about the agents involved in translation and how they relate to the expectations of audiences, while in the same volume – Nelson and Maher's *Perspectives on Literature and Translation: Creation, circulation, reception* (2013) – Sally-Ann Spencer outlines the specific role of literary prizes in influencing what gets translated. The importance of paratexts is a distinct area of interest, with Carolyn Shread (2010) stressing the colonizing role of paratexts, designed to make a foreign culture easier for domestic consumption. When studying translations and their paratexts in the classroom, we can start by asking what the perceived needs and expectations of English-language readers are, where they come from and whether they are changing. Of particular relevance to students today is an understanding of how ideas of difference and otherness are constructed. Emily Apter has observed 'tendencies in world literature [...] toward the celebration of nationally and ethnically branded "differences" that have been niche-marketed as commercial identities' (Apter, 2013, p. 2). Similarly, Graham Huggan (2007, xii), discussing Australia, suggests that what is chosen for translation is 'what is seen abroad as "Australian" in markedly – marketably – stereotypical terms'.

In the Modern Languages classroom, we can deconstruct these identities, taking into account how they have been shaped by a history of power imbalances. The book cover, as a form of paratext, is considered in a 2016 collection of essays edited by Nicole Matthews and Nickianne Moody, while Marco Sonzogni (2011) astutely illustrates the role the book cover plays in translation through a study of multiple editions of Umberto Eco's *The Name of the Rose*. Discussion of book covers from around the world are an easy addition to classroom discussion of a text, even where translation is not the main focus of the class. Moving from the individual book to consider translators and publishers, Helen Vassallo's groundbreaking study *Towards a Feminist Translator Studies: Intersectional Activism in Translation and Publishing* (2022) interrogates unconscious biases in translation and foregrounds the work of translators and independent publishers as activists. At the other end of the translation process, Audience Studies investigates how readers understand and respond to what they read in translation. An interesting example here is the 'Reading Transculturally, Consuming Foreignness? Investigating Reading Fiction in Translation in the West Midlands' project, which ran from 2014 to 2016, led by Danielle Fuller, Angela Kershaw and Gabriela Saldanha at the University of Birmingham. The central concern of the project was 'What kind of foreignness are UK readers willing to consume in the UK in the early 21st century?'[1]

The recent collection *Teaching Literature in Translation: Pedagogical Contexts and Reading Practices*, edited by Brian James Baer and Michelle Woods (2022), focuses on translation

[1] University of Birmingham (n.d.) 'Research', Available from: https://www.birmingham.ac.uk/schools/lcahm/departments/languages/research/projects/translation-projects.aspx (Accessed: 1 March 2023).

literacy, providing numerous examples of how and why translation literacy can be taught in the context of both 'world literature' and 'national' literature courses. Baer suggests that the 'basics of translation literacy' are 'that natural languages are asymmetrical or non-equivalent, that most words are polysemous, and that words, phrases, and linguistic structures bear the traces of previous usage' (2022, p. 5). He adds that once this groundwork has been laid, classes can turn to both the broad context in which a translation is produced and the specific context of the individual text and translator. Baer provides a series of questions and tasks to share with students to improve their translation literacy. The volume then includes reflections on teaching translated literature from across the globe. Of special relevance to my own work is Denise Kripper's chapter on 'teaching *a* Latin American literature' in translation (2022, p. 102, original emphasis). Kripper describes 'foster[ing] a more situated reading of the texts in question, understanding them not only within their contexts of production but also framed as new works with a role to play in the recipient culture' (2022, p. 104). It is worth remembering that the reasons for publishing or reading a certain text in English may differ from the reasons as to why it was published or read in its original language; for example, anglophone readers may be looking for a window into understanding an unfamiliar culture.

'Contemporary Hispanic fiction in translation': A case study of an undergraduate module

As an example of how the study of translations can aid critical reflection on intercultural communication and imaginaries of others, let us consider my module 'Contemporary Hispanic Fiction in Translation', taught to final-year students studying Spanish. To break students out of seeing translations only as texts that move words from one language to another, I encouraged them to compare the translation and reception of texts from different parts of the Spanish-speaking world and to think about the role played by translators, publishers and critics of Hispanic fiction in shaping the imaginaries of Spanish-speaking countries held by English-speaking readers. Our case studies were *Los enamoramientos* (2011) by Javier Marías from Spain, translated as *The Infatuations* by Margaret Jull Costa and published by Penguin (2013); *Arde el monte de noche* (2009) by Juan Tomás Ávila Laurel from Equatorial Guinea, translated as *By Night the Mountain Burns* by Jethro Soutar and published by And Other Stories (2014); and two Mexican novels, *Señales que precederán al fin del mundo* (2009), by Yuri Herrera, translated as *Signs Preceding the End of the World* by Lisa Dillman, also published by And Other Stories (2014), and *La historia de mis dientes* (2013) by Valeria Luiselli, translated as *The Story of My Teeth* by Christina MacSweeney and published by Granta (2015). These texts were chosen to cover a broad geographic range, as well as a range of publishers from the independent to the global conglomerate. Each case study involved close comparative reading of extracts from the source and the translation, and study of paratexts such as marketing materials, interviews, reviews and prizes. The students also presented their own examples and offered analyses of books from Venezuela, Mexico and Chile, as well as moving into the lusophone world with *The Book of Chameleons* (2008) by Angolan writer José Eduardo Agualusa.

As the aim was to get students to challenge their ideas about translation, the course raised far more questions than answers. As Wilson (2013, p. 178) suggests, some key questions to ask are: What are foreign markets acquiring? What agents are dominant? What do readers expect or are taught to expect? There are two sides to take into account here: the source culture and the target culture. Firstly, we considered how Spanish-speaking countries present themselves. This includes national prizes as, in Spencer's words, a form of 'domestic endorsement' (Spencer, 2013, p. 196), and books recommended for translation by cultural institutions (e.g. New Books in Spanish). We explored how, in Spain, the Ministry of Education, Culture and Sports funds translation of Spanish texts, while Acción Cultural Española offers subsidies for Spanish authors, artists and cultural professionals to travel to promote their work. Secondly, we considered how cultural agents in the target language shape imaginaries of these countries, beginning with what is chosen to be translated. Does the choice of books reinforce or challenge national stereotypes? Based on Apter's comments, we discussed cases where books seemed to have been chosen to fulfil a market for 'nationally and ethnically branded "differences"' (2013, p. 2), with attention to how this varies according to the country of origin. We debated whether Spanish writers get to be 'universal' while Latin American or African writers are pressured to reflect or represent their nation in some way.

In this respect, I encouraged students to think about the uneven numbers of books in translation from different countries and what that could mean. From the Three Percent databases of books published in translation each year[2] we see that Spanish is the second most commonly translated language into English, after French, with about 15 per cent of all translations in 2017 (the last year for which there is a complete database). However, of 507 translations from Spanish between 2008 and 2016, while 172 were from Spain and 117 from Argentina, there was none from Paraguay or Panama. Costa Rica, the Dominican Republic, Ecuador, El Salvador, Equatorial Guinea, Puerto Rico and Venezuela had 15 between them. Students were asked to think about reasons for these inequalities. In some ways, they reflect the relative strength or weakness of the national publishing industry in each country, but can they also tell us something about English-speaking readers' levels of interest in different countries? We viewed these statistics in light of Pascale Casanova's definition of translation as 'an act of consecration that gives [works] access to literary visibility and existence' (2004, p. 135). She calls this process 'littérisation' (Casanova, 2004, p. 135), maintaining that it is only by being recognized as worthy of translation by the world literary gatekeepers that writing from peripheral literary nations becomes 'literature'. What does this mean for our ideas about countries with few translations? Does this in turn affect the ways in which people in those countries value (or not) their own writing?

[2] Three Percent and Open Letter Books (n.d.) Welcome to the Translation Database. **https://www.publishersweekly.com/pw/translation/home/index.html (Accessed: 27 February 2023).**

In relation to both the choice of text and the way it is translated, we asked how much the source text and its translation draw attention to linguistic or cultural differences. While John Sturrock argues that 'readers hope not to be reminded as they go that what they are reading is (only) a translation' (2010, p. 51), Rebecca Walkowitz (2015) has coined the term 'born translated' to describe books which both solicit translation and draw attention to translation through their content and style. In reading these texts, we noted the extent to which readers were reminded that they were reading a translation. Moving on to reception, we explored how paratexts, such as cover images, marketing campaigns, notes and introductions, all 'help shed light on how the agents involved in translation – translators, editors, publishers – characterize their audience and assess their needs and expectations in order to ensure the foreign is at once appealing and accessible' (Nelson and Maher, 2013, p. 8). From these paratexts, we assessed how much readers are expected to know about the source culture, how much is explained to them and in what ways. Similarly, we analysed reviews, which have 'the power either to maintain or to subvert stereotypical imaginings of a foreign culture for its readership' (Wilson, 2013, p. 186), and prizes as a form of 'accredited visibility' (Thompson, 2010, p. 276). Students were asked to find reviews of contemporary Hispanic fiction in translation to discuss in class, with attention to recurring terms (like 'magical realism'), how the source culture was presented (if at all), the images used to illustrate the texts, references to other authors, and whether there was any evaluation of the work of the translator (if they were named at all). We asked how translations are valued, and particularly whether it is important for them to be seen to be in some way different or unusual, or representative of their source culture. For our Latin American texts, we interrogated Alberto Fuguet's 2009 claim that publishers were interested in literature from Latin America only if it fitted with the trend for magical realism, with attention to how often the term appears still in reviews of a wide variety of books.

The four case studies raised specific questions about what it means to be 'representative' of a culture. Firstly, in relation *to The*

Infatuations, we discussed how, while authors such as Javier Cercas and Antonio Muñoz Molina have found success in the UK with narratives about the Spanish Civil War, Marías has been lauded in reviews for his 'unique exploration of many themes that obsessed the great literary figures: secrecy, treason, love and the impossibility of definitive knowledge' (The Culture Trip, 2019). We considered whether Marías as a white, European man had more freedom to explore supposedly 'universal' themes without having to represent cultural specificities. The debate between the criticism that Marías has received from critics and intellectuals in Spain 'for not being authentically Spanish' (Herzberger, 2011, p. 2) and Gareth Wood's assertion that his works 'represent a deep and thoughtful engagement with Spain's twentieth-century history and contemporary society' (Wood, 2012, pp. 14–15) prompted us to ask what makes people consider something 'authentically Spanish'.

In terms of the translation, we picked up on comments praising the smoothness of Margaret Jull Costa's translation. Michael Eaude, for example, wrote in his review in *The Independent*, 'You do not notice her presence: when the translator vanishes, it means the translation's good' (2013). We read this in tandem with Steven White's (1997) warning against prioritizing 'smooth' translations for studying literature from other countries, as a form of 'translation imperialism', which gives the false impression that writers around the world simply imitate anglophone writing styles. Marías also provides an instructive example of how the prestige conferred by prizes – or even the hint of prizes – conditions the circulation of texts. We considered the claim that Vintage and Penguin Modern Classics reissuing Marías's back catalogue was 'a bet on his chances of winning the Nobel' (Heyman, 2014).

By contrast, with *By Night the Mountain Burns*, we considered how reviews tended to judge the book as a piece of ethnography. For example, *Publishers Weekly* (2014) wrote:

> **Laurel's approach is ethnographic and uses an islander's first-person perspective to provide brief histories of the culture, terrain, and habitat. Although the narrative**

> voice is sometimes repetitive and intentionally elusive, the descriptions of the island's creatures, customs, language, and lore lead to clever revelations in the plot.

Reviews suggested that readers would look to this book as a way into understanding Equatorial Guinea, reaffirming that readers were expected to have little prior knowledge of the country. In this context, the translator takes on the role of an activist or informer, charged with translating an unknown culture. Before *By Night...*, only one other book had ever been translated from Equatorial Guinea – *Shadows of Your Black Memory* by Donato Ndongo-Bidyogo, written in 1987 and published in translation in 2007. Translator Jethro Soutar wrote in a piece for *Words Without Borders*:

> Having recently translated *By Night the Mountain Burns*, by Juan Tomás Ávila Laurel, I am acutely aware of what a forgotten place Equatorial Guinea is. Whenever I talk about what I've been working on, I'm met with blank looks: most people have never heard of Equatorial Guinea, let alone know that it's Africa's only Spanish-speaking country. (Soutar, 2014)

Studying the book obliged students to think about the ongoing influence of Spanish colonialism. Spain remains a link between Spanish-speaking countries and foreign publishers and yet, according to Ndongo-Bidyogo and Ngom, Spanish publishers prefer to 'traducir a los africanus de habla portuguesa, inglesa o francesa antes que mirar en la terraza de su propia casa' [translate Portuguese-, English- or French-speaking Africans before looking in their own backyard] (Ndongo-Bidyogo and Ngom, 2000, p. 54). In linguistic terms, we looked at how Soutar used language to convey the legacies of Spanish colonialism, keeping words related to religious and educational institutions in Spanish in his translation to allude to these as foundations of colonial power.

Finally, *Signs Preceding the End of the World* and *The Story of My Teeth* allowed us to think about how countries use translation as a form of cultural diplomacy, as the translations of both books in 2015 fitted in with the year of UK/Mexico collaboration and the Mexico focus at the London Book Fair. Authors Yuri Herrera and Valeria Luiselli are part of a group of emerging Mexican literary talent, presented as innovative and cosmopolitan, yet also a source of pride for Mexico. *Signs* was winner of the 2016 Best Translated Book Award – the first Spanish-language writer to win the award for fiction. As well as praising the 'dazzling style', the judges noted that the book 'giv[es] readers an urgent account from today's wall-building world' (Cain, 2016). Reviews and recommendations often explicitly promoted reading the novel as a resistance to US president Donald Trump. We considered how the book challenges the view of Mexican immigrants in the United States, but also how reviews revealed enduring misunderstandings or limited cultural knowledge from English-speaking readers. For example, reviews referred to generic 'magical realism' rather than specific Mayan beliefs, and the fact that the chapter titles reflect the Mayan belief in the journey to Mictlán was missed or misunderstood by reviewers. Comparisons of book covers for translations into multiple languages revealed the predominance of easily recognized symbols for Mexico – cacti and skeletons – with only the Italian cover capturing Mayan iconography.

As for *Teeth*, we explored how Luiselli bucked the trend of the 'narconovela' with a complex, parodic reflection on international art markets and the inflated value given to certain objects that is nonetheless firmly rooted in Mexico City. In an article against tendencies in recent Mexican literary criticism, Luiselli (2012) condemns the obsession with 'the national' instead of considering the text as a work of literature. We considered how, and why, her novel was read by anglophone reviewers in a very different light to Herrera's, with a focus on the 'universal' rather than the national. The book is also an enlightening case study of the role a translator can play in the reception of a text, as translator Christina MacSweeney added an entirely new chapter to help orient readers. This collaboration became a selling point of the novel, with the *New York Times* reviewer claiming, 'There is something thrilling about finding a writer generous enough to invite another to participate in her work' (Krusoe, 2015). This again led us to discussion about how often the translator's mediation in bringing a text to another language and culture is rendered invisible, masking differences between source culture and target culture.

In their final assessments, students were asked to reflect on either how the cultural values of the target language shape the translation process, how translations 'promote cultural understanding and ethical self-reflection' (Berman and Wood, 2005, p. 104), or the different expectations and pressures on various Hispanic writers to be 'representative'. From having had little exposure to translated fiction before the course, by the end the students demonstrated nuanced understanding of these issues and reported rethinking their own reading practices.

Conclusion

The study of translations is a powerful tool for both language learning and intercultural understanding. Through asking students to compare target text and source text, we can encourage them to consider more closely the meanings implicit in words and style, and the cultural specificity of language, thereby developing their translation literacy. Moving beyond the words themselves, though, to look at the choices of books for translation, their paratexts and their reception, prompts reflection on the ways that readers in the target language view the source culture, as well as the influence of the translator, publisher, reviewer and others involved in the process of translation in shaping, reaffirming and challenging cultural imaginaries. As Suzanne Jill Levine, a leading Spanish to English translator, highlights in *The Subversive Scribe*:

> **Readers also need to understand how Latin American writing is transmitted to them and *how* differences and similarities between cultures and languages affect *what* is finally transmitted. Knowing the other and how we receive or hear the other is a fundamental step towards knowing ourselves.** (Levine, 2009, pp. xiv–xv)

Looking at how imaginaries of different countries are shaped by what is chosen for translation and how that is presented to readers helps students to understand how we form and present our own identities and our relationships with others.

References

Agualusa, J. E. (2008) *The Book of Chameleons: A Novel.* Trans. D. Hahn. New York: Simon & Schuster.

Antón, T. de Inés (2020) The significance of translation literacy in the higher education classroom. *The UWI Quality Education Forum*, 24, 174–96.

Apter, E. (2013) *Against World Literature: On the Politics of Untranslatability*. New York: Verso.

Baer, B. J. (2022) Is there a translation in this class?, in Baer, B. J. and Woods, M. (eds), *Teaching Literature in Translation: Pedagogical Contexts and Reading Practices*. London: Routledge, pp. 3–12.

Bassnett, S. and Trivedi, H. (eds) (2012) Introduction: Of colonies, cannibals and vernaculars, in *Postcolonial Translation: Theory and Practice*. London: Routledge.

Berman, S. and Wood, M. (2005) *Nation, Language, and the Ethics of Translation*. Princeton, NJ: Princeton University Press.

Cain, S. (2016) Yuri Herrera wins best translated book award. *The Guardian*, 5 May. Available from: https://www.theguardian.com/books/2016/may/05/yuri-herrera-best-translated-book-award-signs-preceding-the-end-of-the-world (Accessed: 1 March 2023).

Casanova, P. (2004) *The World Republic of Letters.* Trans. M. B. DeBevoise. Cambridge, MA: Harvard University Press.

Eaude, M. (2013) The Infatuations, by Javier Marías, trans. Margaret Jull Costa. *The Independent*, 15 March. Available from: https://www.independent.co.uk/arts-entertainment/books/reviews/the-infatuations-by-javier-marias-trans-margaret-jull-costa-8535070.html (Accessed: 1 March 2023).

Fuguet, A. (2009) Magical neoliberalism. 17 November. Available from: https://foreignpolicy.com/2009/11/17/magical-neoliberalism/ (Accessed: 1 March 2023).

Herzberger, D. K. (2011) *A Companion to Javier Marías*. Woodbridge: Tamesis.

Heyman, S. (2014) Javier Marías: Spain's elegant master novelist. *New York Times*, 25 September. Available from: https://www.nytimes.com/2014/09/26/arts/international/javier-maras-spains-elegant-master-novelist.html (Accessed: 1 March 2023).

Huggan, G. (2007) *Australian Literature: Postcolonialism, racism, transnationalism*. Oxford: Oxford University Press.

Klitgård, I. (2018) Calling for translation literacy. The use of covert translation in student academic writing in higher education. *Translation and Translanguaging in Multilingual Contexts*, 4 (2), 306–23.

Kripper, D. (2022) In English translation: Teaching a Latin American literature, in Baer, B. J. and Woods, M (eds), *Teaching Literature in Translation: Pedagogical contexts and reading practices*. New York: Routledge, pp. 102–10.

Krusoe, J. (2015) 'The Story of My Teeth,' by Valeria Luiselli. *New York Times*, 11 September. Available from: https://www.nytimes.com/2015/09/13/books/review/the-story-of-my-teeth-by-valeria-luiselli.html?smid=url-share (Accessed: 1 March 2023).

Landers, C. E. (1995) Latin America and translation: Three contributions to knowing the other. *Latin American Research Review*, 30 (3), 254–63.

Levine, S. J. (2009) *The Subversive Scribe: Translating Latin American fiction*. London: Dalky Archive.

Luiselli, V. (2012) Novedad de la narrativa mexicana II: Contra las tentaciones de la nueva crítica. 1 February. Available from: https://www.nexos.com.mx/?p=14682 (Accessed: 1 March 2023).

Matthews, N. and Moody, N. (2016) *Judging a Book by Its Cover: Fans, publishers, designers, and the marketing of fiction*. London: Routledge.

Ndongo-Bidyogo, D. (2007) *Shadows of Your Black Memory*. Trans. M. Ugarte. Chicago: Swan Isle Press.

Ndongo-Bidyogo, D. and Ngom, M. (eds) (2000) *Literatura de Guinea Ecuatoria (Antología)*. Madrid: SIAL.

Nelson, B. and Maher, B. (2013) *Perspectives on Literature and Translation: Creation, circulation, reception*. London: Routledge.

Publishers Weekly (2014) By night the mountain burns, n.d. Available from: https://www.publishersweekly.com/978-1-908276-40-7 (Accessed: 1 March 2023).

QAA (2019) *Subject Benchmark Statement: Languages, cultures and societies*. Gloucester: The Quality Assurance Agency for Higher Education.

Schwartz, R. (2019) Bridging the gap. *In Other Words*, 52, 71–8.

Shread, C. (2010) Decolonizing paratexts: Re-presenting Haitian literature in English translations. *Neohelicon*, 37 (1), 113–25.

Sonzogni, M. (2011) *Re-Covered Rose: A case study in book cover design as intersemiotic translation*. Amsterdam: John Benjamins Publishing.

Soutar, J. (2014) New writing from Equatorial Guinea: An introduction. *Writing without Borders*, 1 June. Available from: http://www.wordswithoutborders.org/article/new-writing-from-equatorial-guinea-an-introduction (Accessed: 1 March 2023).

Spencer, S.-A. (2013) Prizing translation: Book awards and literary translation, in Nelson, B. and Maher, B. (eds), *Perspectives on Literature and Translation: Creation, circulation, reception*. London: Routledge.

Sturrock, J. (2010) Writing between the lines: The language of translation, in Baker, M. (ed), *Critical Readings in Translation Studies*. London: Routledge, pp. 49–64.

The Culture Trip (2019) 10 of the best contemporary Spanish authors. *The Culture Trip*, 18 December. Available from: https://theculturetrip.com/europe/spain/articles/the-voice-of-spain-10-of-the-best-contemporary-spanish-authors/ (Accessed: 1 March 2023).

Thompson, J. B. (2010) *Merchants of Culture: The publishing business in the twenty-first century*. Cambridge: Polity Press.

Vassallo, H. (2022) *Towards a Feminist Translator Studies: Intersectional activism in translation and publishing*. London: Routledge.

Venuti, L. (ed) (2017) *Teaching Translation: Programs, courses, pedagogies*. London: Routledge.

Venuti, L. (1995) *The Translator's Invisibility: A history of translation*. London: Routledge.

Walkowitz, R. L. (2015) *Born Translated: The contemporary novel in the age of world literature*. New York: Columbia University Press.

Wells, N., Forsdick, C., Bradley, J., Burdett, C., Burns, J., Demossier, M., de Zárate, M. H., Huc-Hepher, S., Jordan, S., Pitman, T. and Wall, G. (2019) Ethnography and modern languages. *Modern Languages Open*, 1. DOI: http://doi.org/10.3828/mlo.v0i0.242.

White, S. (1997) Translation and teaching: The dangers of representing Latin America for students in the United States. *Cadernos de Tradução*, 1 (2), 87–97.

Wilson, R. (2013) Terra Australis Incognita even now? The reception of Australian literature in Italian translation, in Nelson, B. and Maher, B. (eds), *Perspectives on Literature and Translation: Creation, circulation, reception*. London: Routledge, pp. 178–94.

Wood, G. J. (2012) *Javier Marías's Debt to Translation: Sterne, Browne, Nabokov*. Oxford: Oxford University Press.

4

Advocacy and collaboration: Stanley Burnshaw's *The Poem Itself*

Tom Boll

Overview

This chapter draws on approaches from genetic criticism and the sociology of collaboration to investigate how Stanley Burnshaw advocated for a method of 'truly literal' translation and commentary in his anthology *The Poem Itself* (1960). Burnshaw's archive provides insight into the relations between concept, practice and the dynamics of social interaction in collaborative translation. The concept of literal translation offered a commonly accepted term that was subject nevertheless to variable interpretation by both Burnshaw and his contributors over the course of the project. His initial proposal and specimen contribution on Stéphane Mallarmé's 'Don du poème' prioritized syntax ahead of other verbal features. His subsequent editing of German contributions focused instead on semantic implication at the expense of syntax. At each of these stages, conflicts of interpretation led to a published text that aggregated competing views rather than resolving them. Burnshaw's later translations of Mallarmé with Henri Peyre reached a stable agreement about the practical application of the concept of literal translation. This agreement led to a more coherent text but persisted with a tendency to record verbal features rather than to account for their function within a reading experience.

Introduction

When *The Poem Itself* was published by Pelican Books in 1964, the back cover announced that its editor, Stanley Burnshaw, had 'found a way to let the English reader grasp the sounds and rhythms of foreign poetry, and not merely the sense' (Burnshaw, 1964).[1] Offered as a form of primer in poetic modernism, the anthology presented a selection of poems in French, German, Spanish, Portuguese, Italian and Russian from the previous 150 years, each accompanied by a prose translation and commentary. Sixty years later, a reader picking up the anthology might be underwhelmed by the claims on its jacket. The casual reference to 'merely the sense' passes hastily over the interpretative work of the translator. Burnshaw's title hardly helps, with its promise of the poem itself, recalling W. K. Wimsatt and M. C. Beardsley's notorious claim in 'The Intentional Fallacy' (1946) that if a poet has succeeded 'then the poem itself shows what he was trying to do' (1954, p. 4). The title seems to date the anthology as a period piece from a time when the New Criticism held sway, concealing its value-laden interpretative gestures behind a claim that the poem was self-sufficient.

If *The Poem Itself* looks dated, a reflection of its time and a certain critical hegemony, the records of its production, held in the Stanley Burnshaw collection at the Harry Ransom Center (University of Texas at Austin), tell a more complex story. The title was a late addition to the project; Burnshaw's initial proposal sternly warned potential contributors to avoid 'New-Critical discussions,

[1] *The Poem Itself* had previously been published in the United States by Holt, Rinehart and Winston in 1960.

I am grateful to the University of East Anglia for funding the research for this essay with a Faculty of Arts and Humanities Small Award; to Harry Ransom Center, The University of Texas at Austin, the Stanley Burnshaw Estate and Daniel Fitts for permission to quote from material in the Stanley Burnshaw Papers at the Harry Ransom Center and *The Poem Itself*; to staff at the Harry Ransom Center for their assistance; and to Birgit Breidenbach for reading a draft version of this essay.

sectarian interpretations, or anything more than what a reader actually requires if he is to get to the poem' (Burnshaw, n.d.i). As his warning suggests, Burnshaw, a poet and publisher, stood at a distance from the academic world inhabited by his contributors. He was mistrustful of the practices, abilities, vanities and pet obsessions of people on whom he nevertheless relied to provide the translations and commentaries for his anthology.

Burnshaw's correspondence reveals repeated acts of advocacy as he attempted to formulate and direct the work of associate editors and individual contributors who did not always share his views about the principles and practices of the anthology, what he described as its 'method' (1964, p. xi). That advocacy was performed across kindred but nevertheless distinct cultural and institutional settings of the commercial publishing house and academe. Burnshaw was not always well disposed to his contributors, complaining after an 'unspeakable' visit to the Modern Language Association annual conference, where he went to seek recruits, that 'never had I taken in so much hot air' (Burnshaw, 1959a). The method of *The Poem Itself* was not 'found', as its blurb claimed, but worked for, produced in an extended process that involved explanation, cajolery, persuasion and negotiation. That process was both cultural, involving ideas about translation and poetic tradition, and social, as Burnshaw attempted to promote a collaborative enterprise that involved over 20 contributors.

Translation is typically a collaborative activity, which is shaped by diverse hands (Cordingley and Frigau Manning, 2017, p. 1; Cordingley, 2020, p. 210). Michael P. Farrell has produced detailed studies of the dynamics of social interaction in artistic collaboration. He sees a rise of 'pseudo-kinship groups' among artists with increased urbanization in the nineteenth century (2001, p. 12), which create their own ad hoc social relations, a pattern of behaviour that is shared by other disciplines such as science and politics (2001, p. 2). He provides a model for articulating the types of exchange that are involved in a project like *The Poem Itself*, where Burnshaw's textual proposition becomes involved in varied forms of social relation. Farrell defines a collaborative circle as:

> A primary group consisting of peers who share similar occupational goals and who, through long periods of dialogue and collaboration, negotiate a common vision that guides their work. The vision consists of a shared set of assumptions about their discipline, including what constitutes good work, how to work, what subjects are worth taking on, and how to think about them. (2001, p. 11)

The group's vision encompasses a range of intellectual positions, practical ('how to work') and theoretical ('how to think about') subjects. Farrell opens out social elements of advocacy, such as dialogue and collaboration, which are involved in establishing this vision. A vision is not simply shared from the outset (or 'found' as the blurb of *The Poem Itself* claimed) but created and put into practice over an extended period. Advocacy here involves both a cause and the ways that someone creates the social relations that will help them to further that cause. Farrell elaborates on typical stages of this process and the dynamics that are involved in them. Collaborations typically begin with 'a balanced exchange process' of work or self-disclosure 'characterized by reciprocity and gradual escalation of both critical and supportive interaction' (2001, p. 152). These exchanges perform a variety of functions. They serve to 'validate one another's identities as serious professionals' (2001, p. 152), allowing members to build trust (2001, p. 123) and 'evolve norms that encourage open communication and wide-ranging exchanges' (2001, p. 20), leading in the most successful cases to a stage of 'instrumental intimacy' characterized by a 'merging of cognitive processes' (2001, p. 23).

Farrell focuses on the microsocial aspects of cultural collaboration, showing how acts of advocacy are drawn into interpersonal relations and negotiations which then shape artistic products. Members of a group can take on executive (2001, p. 24) but also more informal roles, which establish 'relatively stable patterns of behaviour that come to be expected of each member' (2001, p. 21). The translation method of *The Poem Itself* was developed through exchanges between Burnshaw and his associate editors on the volume, Dudley Fitts and Henri Peyre, and put into practice by over 20 contributors who were answerable to their section editors and, in some cases, directly to Burnshaw himself. The executive arrangements for each section varied, meaning that Burnshaw was involved with individual contributors in different ways.

Burnshaw's papers hold substantial records of these exchanges, revealing different attitudes to translation and different construals of Burnshaw's proposition, which resisted, diverted and transformed his intentions. Genetic Criticism, which emerged from the Institut des textes et manuscrits modernes (ITEM) in Paris, founded by Louis Hay in 1968, provides methods for organizing, classifying and analysing this archival material. Genetic critics make a methodological distinction between the genetic dossier and the *avant-texte* of a published work. The genetic dossier is defined by Jean Bellemin-Noël as 'the collection of documents that have been used for the writing of a work', arranged by the critic in the sequential order of its production (1977, p. 9).[2] This is a work of assemblage and classification that provides the basis for the construction of the *avant-texte*. The *avant-texte* is 'a particular reconstruction of what preceded a text, established by a critical approach with the help of a specific methodology' (1977, p. 9); that is, it subjects the assemblage and classification of the genetic dossier to critical interpretation. For Pierre-Marc de Biasi, the *avant-texte* has no existence 'outside the critical discourse that produces it' (de Biasi, 2004, p. 43). Genetic Criticism does not offer an all-inclusive critical approach, or 'recipes' for analysis (Bellemin-Noël, 1977, p. 9); instead, it provides a method for making archival material available for further critical approaches that will bring specific questions to bear on it.

Genetic critics have produced sophisticated methods for classifying the archival material of the genetic dossier. De Biasi provides a detailed typology of genetic documentation, relating specific document types to different stages of the writing process – provisional, exploratory, preparatory, structuring, research and compositional. These stages provide a way of accounting for

[2] My translation.

shifting configurations of conceptualization and the activity of writing, or 'textualization', over the course of a project (de Biasi, 1996, pp. 34–5).

The holdings for *The Poem Itself* at the Harry Ransom Center are substantial: 62 folders in five boxes contain material by Burnshaw, his associate editors, contributors and typesetter, comprising handwritten, typewritten and mimeographed letters, proposals, outlines, plans, schedules, notes, a specimen contribution, drafts and proofs. The material is organized according to a loose operational logic in folders dedicated to preliminary correspondence, financial correspondence, general correspondence, page proofs by language, individual poets, some individual translators and the appendix.

This organization cuts across the chronology of the work's production, obscuring a narrative of its development. A chronological dossier of the material reveals that the main genesis of *The Poem Itself* took place in two stages. An initial pre-compositional phase was dedicated to conceiving, planning, recruiting for and providing an initial determination of the project. This stage involved a proposal, a specimen contribution on Stéphane Mallarmé's 'Don du poème' and the responses of potential collaborators. There followed the compositional phase involving the selection of poets and poems, and editorial exchanges over successive drafts of the contributions. While this phase involved the textualization of the initial proposal, it also carried through debates about the conceptualization of the project and the relation of conceptualization to practice. Each of these phases involved shifting forms of advocacy on Burnshaw's part as the project developed and examples of compliance and resistance on the part of his contributors.

The relation of conceptualization to textualization, or practice, is a persistent concern of Genetic Criticism, whether openly stated, as in de Biasi's typology, or as a metaphorical implication of its critical vocabulary. Daniel Ferrer's notorious statement that a manuscript is an 'operational protocol' for making a text (2011, p. 43) attempts to extrapolate the status of principle and guideline from the raw material of textual genesis. De Biasi employs similarly connoted metaphors of politics and power, as a draft stage of textualization becomes a 'regulatory and causal authority' for a project, which will 'police all further transformation of its form by the activation of its own controls' (1996, p. 30). The correspondence in which Burnshaw and his contributors articulate and dispute textual choices and principles makes forms of guideline explicit. These exchanges provide direct evidence of conceptualization, of cultural ideas about poetry and translation. They also present strong implicit evidence of social interaction, as Burnshaw and his interlocutors negotiate the passage of their beliefs and interpretations through draft stages to the published anthology. Ferrer and de Biasi employ metaphors to extrapolate power struggles from single-author manuscripts – protocols and authority are established that can police and control the direction of a project. Burnshaw's papers present actual struggles for power between different actors. They reveal the ways in which his advocacy for the project becomes embroiled in different forms of social relation and competing cultural ideas and practices.

Classification of the different phases of the genetic dossier allows one to place the exchanges between Burnshaw and his contributors in a chronological sequence. In order to make that narrative critically meaningful, however, to allow the genetic dossier to speak as an *avant-texte*, I wish to unpack that process in terms of social and cultural questions. Drawing on critical approaches from the sociology of artistic collaboration and reflection on the concept of 'literal' translation, I will ask: How does Burnshaw define his project in theory and in practice at different stages? And how do social interactions with his collaborators shape the published work? My aim is to show how Burnshaw's advocacy for the project, and the adoption and transformation of that advocacy by his contributors, interwove cultural beliefs about text and translation with executive and personal social relations.

Conceptualization and recruitment

Burnshaw first approached potential contributors for the anthology in February 1958, sending a letter and mimeographed proposal

(Burnshaw, n.d.i) to Harry Levin and Dudley Fitts in the hope that they would take charge of the French and Spanish-Latin American sections respectively (Burnshaw, 1958a; 1958b). Levin was an academic specialist in comparative literature based at Harvard, Fitts a sometime poet and active translator, who had produced *An Anthology of Contemporary Latin American Poetry* (1942). This opening contact with Levin and Fitts provided an account of the project's initial formulation, situating it as a response to encounters with a succession of previous publications and practices. Burnshaw recounted his 'frustrated experiences' with an environment in which 'there was virtually no concern with literal faithfulness; translations of poems were "recreations" by a translator poet who could do almost anything he fancied' (1958a). He decided that 'the only feasible way of getting to poems in a language that one didn't command was by learning to pronounce (only approximately, of course) the lines of the original and "simultaneously" reading a truly literal translation'. Yet 'truly' literal translations proved hard to come by. Citing editions of Mallarmé, published by New Directions, and Rainer Maria Rilke, translated by C. F. MacIntyre, he concluded that it seemed difficult for even 'literal translators to stay literal. Their EARS and IMAGINATIONS tend to push them towards breaking the rule [...] and into changing the sentence structure of the original.' Aside from the problems of literal translation (and translators), Burnshaw also concluded that further explanation would be necessary to guide the reader to the poem. The Penguin series of national poetry anthologies, which accompanied the source texts with what it described as 'plain prose translations' (Cohen, 1958, title page), could be 'strange and forbidding'. He therefore turned for a further model to Wallace Fowlie's critical book on Mallarmé (1953) where 'the literal translation alone will not move any but the most zealous reader to within reach of the poems'. If he was to get to the poems, 'he must read the literal translations together with Fowlie's interpretative comments' (1958a).

Raymonde Debray Genette (1979) has established a distinction between 'endogenesis', the process of writing, and 'exogenesis', sources that are external to a writing project but which nevertheless contribute to it. For de Biasi, these sources offer 'dialogic elements, which give a motivational and heuristic kick-start to the endogenetic process' (1996, p. 46). Burnshaw offered his potential collaborators a thorough account of the exogenetic impetus for his project, the sources he was reacting to, modifying and adapting. This account performed both a conceptual and a social function. Farrell notes that collaborative projects form around a shared hostility to established practices: they are not merely innovative but reactive, 'provocative toward those in authority' (2001, p. 14). Burnshaw invited his contributors to join a cultural-political intervention in current translation practice. His proposal began to clarify what that intervention involved conceptually. His interest in the source poem focused more on sound than on semantic content. He also took a step towards clarifying the formal criteria of his 'truly literal' translation as primarily a concern for syntax ('the sentence structure of the original poem'). Both in terms of work to which he was reacting and detail of conception, the translations received greater attention than the commentaries at this stage, which would act as a form of supplement to help the reader engage with the translations.

The social exchanges that shaped *The Poem Itself* turned on a cultural argument around what Burnshaw described as his 'truly literal' translation method. While literalism has been a persistent concern throughout the history of translation, it has also been a mercurial one, a 'relative' term (Shuttleworth and Cowie, 2014, p. 95) which 'has meant different things to different people' (Chesterman, 2017, p. 238). Andrew Chesterman produces a working definition of literal translation that is contingent upon the priorities of the translator: 'literal translation is one that is formally closer to its source than some other translation of the same source chunk, on given criteria' (2017, p. 240). The description 'literal' will be meaningful only once one has established criteria of the formal properties one wishes a given literal translation to prioritize, relative to other possible or actual translations.

This 'comparative' perspective (Chesterman, 2017, p. 240) is implicit in a number of accounts of literal translation, which use the term to distinguish between different stages of the translation process. For J. C. Catford, literal translation 'may start, as it were, from a word-for-word translation, but makes changes in conformity with TL grammar' (1965, p. 25), while Birgitta Dimitrova sees it as a way of 'playing it safe' in a first or intermediate draft (2005, p. 53). Literal translation is never entirely present – it is something aimed for or (more commonly in these accounts) something that is being left behind. For Douglas Robinson, 'most so called literal translations are in fact compromises with the ideal' (1998, p. 125), while George Steiner describes it as 'the least attainable' of all approaches (1992, p. 324). Burnshaw's advocacy for a 'truly literal' translation is thus a quixotic project, but not a meaningless one. It provides an impetus for the anthology as a reaction to existing practice but without providing a stable definition and criteria. Its manifestations in practice will shift as one moves from Burnshaw to his associate editors and contributors, and from one stage of the project to another.

The initial reaction to Burnshaw's proposal was lukewarm: Levin did not feel qualified to contribute while Fitts thought its sonic concern was a 'fallacy' (Levin, 1958; Fitts, 1958a). Burnshaw persisted nevertheless with a specimen contribution on Mallarmé's 'Don du poème', which he sent out to Fitts, Levin and Henri Peyre, a French scholar at Yale and President of the Modern Language Association whom Levin had suggested as his replacement. The specimen provided a concrete example of how the theoretical proposition might work in practice. Burnshaw invited Peyre to compare his translation to the prose version that appeared in *The Penguin Book of French Verse* (Burnshaw, 1958c). A comparison of the opening lines in the two translations gives an early indication of the form and priorities of Burnshaw's 'truly literal' translation method.

> Je t'appporte l'enfant d'une nuit d'Idumée!
> Noire, à l'aile saignante et pâle, déplumée,
> Par le verre brûlé d'aromates et d'or,
> Par les carreaux glacés, hélas! mornes encor
> L'aurore se jeta sur la lampe angélique [...] (Burnshaw, n.d.ii)

I bring you the child of an Idumean night! Dark, with bleeding wing and pale, its feathers plucked, through the glass burned with spices and gold, through the icy panes, still dreary, alas! the dawn threw itself on the angelic lamp. (Hartley, 1965, p. 189)

(1) I bring you the child (offspring) of an Idumean night. (2) Black (dark), with wing bleeding and pale, (its feathers) plucked, (3) Through the window burnt with spices and gold, (4) Through the icy panes, alas, still bleak (dreary), (5) Dawn hurled itself upon the angelic lamp. (Burnshaw, n.d.ii)

One can see that Burnshaw's translation is similar to Hartley's for Penguin. The most conspicuous innovation is his use of brackets, which perform a variety of functions: to indicate a figurative expansion of the denotative translation, as in '(offspring)'; to mark off explanatory insertions that clarify syntax, as in '(its feathers)'; and to offer alternative translations, as in '(dreary)'. There is a less discriminating tendency to use brackets to hedge his bets, preserving some of Hartley's choices, such as 'dark' and 'its feathers', but subordinating them to his own choices. Burnshaw also makes a more persistent effort to calque syntax, replicating Mallarmé's post-modifier with 'wing bleeding' and the position of *hélas* in line 4.

The accompanying commentary discussed 'Don du poème' in terms of Mallarmé's verse drama *Hérodiade*, perhaps taking a lead from the account in Fowlie (1953, p. 142), and drew on key statements of Mallarmé's poetic theory such as '"To paint not the thing but the effect it produces"' (Burnshaw, n.d.ii). He provided a setting for the poem's narrative action and an explanation of principal themes such as the poet's fear of creative impotence. Aside from a passing reference to 'indefiniteness' of punctuation, formal features received scant attention.

Responses to the specimen were detailed and unsparing. Peyre acknowledged that the translation replicated the syntax and movement of the poem but not its music, rhythm or the 'rare effects of its words'. The commentary read 'like a paraphrasis', failing to reflect on rhythm and various semantic features: the suggestiveness of words, images and the recurrence of familiar lexical items (Peyre, 1958a). Fitts found the translation 'risible in the extreme' and the commentary a paraphrase, chiding Burnshaw, 'it is naughty of you to dismiss the real difficulties [...] "cold feet", "angelical" (dawn? or the lamp?), the odd shift from passé défini to indéfini; the whole damn AURA of the poem' (Fitts, 1958b). Peyre wondered, 'Is the conception of the work as a whole sound, practically speaking?' (Peyre, 1958a).

Peyre's observation, that the translation replicated the syntax of the poem but not its other features, presented an early example of the troublesome conceptual ambiguity of Burnshaw's 'truly literal' translation. Burnshaw had satisfied one formal criterion but not a host of others that were valued by one of his potential contributors. Peyre's objection also raised questions about the status of the translation, which entails consequences for the reader's approach to it. For Lionel Trilling, the translation of *The Poem Itself* has a clear status: it 'frankly avows its merely ancillary intention' as a route to reading a foreign language (1984, p. 96). However, Clive Scott has challenged the view that translation can ever be truly ancillary in this manner. In an analysis of Francis Scarfe's Baudelaire translations for Penguin of 1964, he observes that, while prose translations 'usually make no claims to ontological independence' (2000, p. 147), they nevertheless cannot avoid embodying various formal devices, such as punctuation, rhythm and syntax, which generate literary effects (2000, pp. 149–50). The Penguin prose translations of poetry, which provided a model for Burnshaw, were commonly nudged in different formal and interpretative directions. Michael Hamburger sometimes attempted to reproduce Hölderlin's metrical effects 'where the rhythm or meter of a line seemed inseparable from what it states' and Hartley adopted 'as literal a rendering as is compatible with reasonable English prose', conceding that a poet like Mallarmé 'is bound to impose an interpretation', which led to a 'more approximate' practice (Hartley, 1965, p. xxxviii).

A 'truly literal' translation is hard to pin down, and Burnshaw found himself confronted at the outset of his project with objections to his choice of criteria and his reluctance to acknowledge the ontological independence of his translation, the types of verbal experience that it embodied.

The criticisms of Peyre and Fitts extended to ways that the commentary accounted for verbal experience. Burnshaw responded to Peyre's suggestions by appending them to a revised version of his commentary. Objections to the translation were answered in part by a paragraph that largely repeated Peyre's observations, declaring that 'some of our English equivalents are too bare' (Burnshaw, n.d.iii). Yet these Peyre additions are oddly stubborn chunks of text, literally stuck on the end of the earlier version with tape. They enumerate rather than evoke or explain the areas of the poem that Peyre felt required more attention.

Nevertheless, both Peyre and Fitts agreed to collaborate on the project as associate editors. A practical model for the anthology had been established, at least provisionally, but the specimen remained an equivocal document: Peyre and Fitts acquiesced to the method of translation, but their criticisms remained unanswered with the commentary a clunky cut-and-paste response to Peyre that relied heavily on paraphrase and a truncated account of the semantic evocation of Mallarmé's language. The revised model was a precarious compromise that left divergent views about the poem and its translation unresolved.

Antagonistic textualization: Burnshaw, Hugo, Jaszi and Sebba

I will now focus on exchanges between Burnshaw and the contributors to the German and French sections. Burnshaw worked out his method in these parts of the anthology. The advocacy represented by the specimen entry on Mallarmé's 'Don du poème' was tested, extended and adapted as new hands took on Burnshaw's proposition with a wider variety of poems.

These exchanges provide evidence of competing practices and conceptualizations of the project. They also reveal different forms of social interaction. Burnshaw came to a working agreement with Fitts and Peyre on 'Don du poème', which acted as a provisional compromise but hardly dispelled substantial doubts about his method. Burnshaw would then launch into the project with German contributors who had not been part of these early discussions.

Correspondence for the German contributions to *The Poem Itself* is concentrated in the period December 1958 to September 1959, immediately following Fitts and Peyre's approval of the Mallarmé specimen in October 1958 (Peyre, 1958b). This section of the anthology was the least settled in terms of executive arrangements and personal relations. Burnshaw trusted his associate editors for French (Henri Peyre) and Spanish–Portuguese (Dudley Fitts), drawing on the relations that they had established through the conceptualization of the project. When John Frederick Nims was brought in as a Spanish contributor and associate editor for the Italian section, Burnshaw wrote approvingly that he was 'excellent in Italian and Spanish' (Burnshaw, 1959b). Burnshaw was less convinced by Howard Hugo, however, who took care of the German section, stripping him of his associate editorship after exasperated exchanges ('you delaying bastard') (Burnshaw, 1959h). Burnshaw had a greater direct involvement in editing the contributions for the German section than he did for Spanish–Portuguese and Italian. He was less familiar with these contributors than with his associate editors and the discrepancy between his knowledge and their expertise was also wider. While Burnshaw worked directly with French, he confessed to Gregor Sebba that he was relying on the German dictionary and 'my own imagination' for the Rilke contributions (1959f). His exchanges reveal competing ideas about how the contributions should be produced at a point where he and his collaborators were still working out what the early conceptualization of the project meant in practice.

Burnshaw's editorial interventions at this stage concentrated on the translations ahead of the commentaries. One of the chief methods for promoting his reading of text and translation was to introduce parenthetical insertions, as he had done for the Mallarmé specimen. One can see his approach illustrated in his comments on a short passage of Hugo von Hofmannsthal's 'Die Beiden' ('The Two') where an unnamed male protagonist is described riding a horse:

> Er ritt auf einem jungen Pferde,
> Und mit nachlässiger Gebärde
> Erzwang er, daß es zitternd stand. (Burnshaw, 1964, p. 134)

The typescript shows the initial translation of these lines by Andrew O. Jaszi, a professor of German at the University of California, Berkeley:

> (6) He rode upon a young horse, (7) And with a negligent gesture (8) He forced it to halt trembling. (Jaszi, n.d.)

Burnshaw made the following suggestions for amendments to the choice of 'negligent' in a letter:

> Line 7: 'nachlässiger' might also suggest careless or quite careless, might it not? A 'negligent gesture' in English isn't quite right. The weight of the word would seem to be 'offhand' in the sense of something that didn't require effort, thought, etc. It was all so simple etc. If I read this right, you ought to introduce 'effortless' or 'careless' somewhere in this line, either in parenthesis (suggest its alternate equivalent) or in square brackets (suggesting its force by explanation). Thus: 'And with a careless [lit. negligent, suggesting effortlessness].' (Burnshaw, n.d. iv)

Burnshaw's response to this one word indicates an approach to 'truly' literal translation that focuses on semantic implication. The results are expansive. Although he describes 'negligent' as not 'quite right', he nevertheless proposes to preserve it in brackets along with further explanation. There is uncertainty at this stage about how Burnshaw wishes to use these brackets. He suggests enclosing 'effortless' or 'careless' in brackets but then his example presents 'careless' as the primary translation with other options (his own and Jaszi's) subordinated parenthetically. The status of the additions is further complicated by the suggestion that they can either be presented as alternative semantic implications (in parenthesis) or as explanation (in square brackets). For a method that aimed to deliver readers to an experience of poetry, these are quite different orders of engagement with the particularity of the text.

This expansive focus on one aspect of the text, its semantic implication, has consequences for another textual feature that had been a formal priority of the specimen Mallarmé contribution: syntax. One can see these competing priorities at work in Burnshaw's suggestion for the final line of the sequence:

> **As for line 8, might 'quivering' be added to trembling, in parenthesis? There is something about trembling that carries the idea of extreme shock to the horse. Quivering has something less of this shock, and the horse becomes less focal, as it were; the limelight remains where it should be, on the man.** (Burnshaw, n.d.v)

Burnshaw suggests that the fearful implication of 'trembling', which focuses on the horse, can be mitigated by a parenthetical insertion of 'quivering', which will then redirect the focus of the phrase to the gesture of the man rather than the horse. The line would thus read, 'He forced it to halt trembling (quivering)', preserving Jaszi's reversal of the German word order in which adverb precedes verb. This suggestion presents the two terms 'trembling' and 'quivering' within a specific syntactic arrangement, which carries implications for the ways one might read the line. One can read parenthetical insertions syntactically in different ways: this and that meaning; this particular aspect of that meaning; this or that meaning; this rather than that meaning.

When a reader encounters brackets, they are left to work out these relations. If they do manage to arrive at Burnshaw's suggestion that the parenthetical 'quivering' tempers the 'extreme shock' of 'trembling', it will take them time. This use of the bracket as a form of qualification or afterthought then truncates the implication that the reader might have derived from 'trembling', correcting it as an incomplete or misleading word choice. The reader is asked to do a lot of work on the ways in which the horse is evoked, and it is doubtful whether the parenthetical clarification then helps direct attention to the man. Clive Scott argues that a prose translation that makes no claims to 'ontological independence', that would 'rather not have to exist', 'falsifies, even if unwittingly, its own capacities' (Scott, 2000, pp. 147 and 154). Prose translation embodies meaning in textual forms, whether it wants to or not. If it aims for the status of a glossary, it will 'remain inert at the textual level' (p. 155). In the case of Burnshaw's use of brackets, which favour semantic implication at the expense of syntax, the result is not so much inert as expansively, intricately involved for the reader.

The example from 'Die Beiden' grapples with a relatively unremarkable piece of German text. It indicates the proliferative nature of Burnshaw's method, the ways in which its expansive attention to semantic implication burdens the syntax of the translation. The different word choices of Burnshaw and his contributor are not so much negotiated as accumulated, leading to an accretive textual process that is hard work for the reader at the receiving end of it. The translations of Rilke presented a more challenging textual example and a starker conflict between Burnshaw and his contributor. With Howard Hugo a negligent associate editor, Burnshaw had to deal directly with the German contributors. He wrote to Hugo to say that he would edit Gregor Sebba, who was providing the Rilke translations and commentaries (Burnshaw, 1959c), confiding that he was worried about his contributions, which were 'skimpy of speculative and discursive comment' (Burnshaw, 1959b). Mistrustful of his academic contributors, Burnshaw was then liable to push his readings hard. That mistrust was reciprocated, meaning that

Sebba was disposed to push back and Burnshaw would later refer to their 'furious correspondence' (Burnshaw, 1959h).

When Sebba sent Burnshaw what he described as a 'rather rough' translation of the first of Rilke's *Duineser Elegien* (*Duino Elegies*) (Sebba, n.d.), Burnshaw replied that he had 'labored over the literal translation in an effort to improve it' (Burnshaw, 1959f). Sebba sets out some of the challenges of the *Elegies* at the start of his commentary:

> Even the German reader must struggle with their uncommon use of common words, with their sentences that tear open to let displaced parts of speech press into the gap, with their obscure allusions and mystifying or wildly farfetched metaphors. (Burnshaw, 1964, p. 153)

Translation and commentary would have to confront a wide range of challenging stylistic detail: non-standard use of everyday lexis, unconventional syntax, private allusions and cryptic figurative language. Sebba quotes Rilke's own characterization of his poetry as a language of '"condensation and abbreviation"' (Burnshaw, 1964, p. 153). In the following passage, Rilke confronts a lack of consolation in divine, human and animal spheres:

> Und so verhalt ich mich denn und verschlucke den Lockruf
> dunkelen Schluchzens. Ach, wen vermögen
> wir denn zu brauchen? Engel nicht, Menschen nicht,
> und die findigen Tiere merken es schon,
> daß wir nicht sehr verläßlich zu Haus sind
> in der gedeuteten Welt. (Burnshaw, 1964, p. 150)

Burnshaw's edited version took the following form:

> (8) Wherefore (and so) I **constrain** myself [hold my breath] and swallow down the call-note (9) of deep-dark sobbing. Alas, whom, after all are we able **to use [turn**

> **to]?** Not angels, not men. (11) and the **wisely perceptive (knowing)** animals do indeed notice (12) that we are not very **trustingly** at home (13) within our interpreted world [the world as we human beings understand it]. (Burnshaw, 1959g)

Sebba's response to this edit amounted to a comprehensive and detailed rejection of Burnshaw's reading of the German and aspects of his translation method. I have highlighted the choices that he contested in bold above. Burnshaw had misread the literal, denotative meaning of words in line 8 '(literally: I hold myself in check; it seems to me that "contain" comes nearer to it than "constrain")' and line 12, which confused *sich verlassen* ('means indeed: "to trust somebody or something"') with *verlässlich* ('means reliable, worthy of being trusted because one is dependable') (Sebba, 1959). Burnshaw's interpretation of individual lexical items obscured higher-order semantic considerations such as tone: '"findig" means resourceful, clever, shrewd, knowing one's way about, being nobody's fool. There is an undertone of irony here.' Burnshaw's use of brackets in line 10 was a distraction ('I would omit "turn to", because it deflects from the principal meaning'). Shortly after this passage in line 18, Burnshaw's use of brackets for an explanatory insertion upset the tone which could be conveyed without the intrusion: 'Here is one place where the elegiac tone of the poem can come through by a verbatim translation. "Oh, and (then also) night, the night..." sacrifices the tone for an explanation which the comment will make anyway' (Sebba, 1959). Sebba's corrections to Burnshaw's editing stretched across the extent of the translation.

Burnshaw's reaction revealed moments of pique: 'I disagree with you completely and totally and quite unperturbed by the Oxford dictionary' (Burnshaw, 1959i). Sebba challenged Burnshaw's reading of the German text, his choice of English to render that reading and his use of brackets. Burnshaw's response was to double down on them. For most of Sebba's objections to the previous example (to 'constrain', 'wisely perceptive (knowing)' and 'trustingly') Burnshaw suggested the inclusion of matter in brackets rather than conceding entirely to Sebba's suggestions: 'I suggest you include in square brackets [literally hold myself] and of course also keep your word "contain"'; 'why not put in square brackets that they see through us. "Shrewd" is not sufficient, I feel'; 'how about doing this "...are not very reliably (trustworthily) at home"?' (Burnshaw, 1959i). Burnshaw's suggestions either incorporated Sebba's explanation for his choices into the translation or acted as a compromise, preserving his own choice which Sebba had rejected, as in the case of 'trustworthily'.

Burnshaw's use of brackets can be understood as a form of advocacy for his 'truly literal' translation method. It attempts to account for the polysemy of lexical items, albeit at the expense of the reader's syntactic experience, the ways that meaning unfolds in a temporal verbal sequence, which had been one of the priorities of the anthology's initial conception. Within the broader method, however, there is a further, more personal advocacy at work, a determination to find ways of representing Burnshaw's own interpretation of the text, based on the dictionary and his 'imagination', in spite of the objections of his contributor. It represents a translation method and a social impasse, a reluctance to broker the gap between different points of view. Farrell describes a 'merging of cognitive processes' (2001, p. 23) as the end point of successful artistic collaboration. Burnshaw's use of brackets maintained a form of cognitive antagonism, leaving a textual record of competing interpretations. In the published version, many of his suggestions were abandoned. Yet expansive and explanatory brackets still proliferate here and elsewhere in the German section, leading to a cluttered experience for the reader.

'Sample "attacks"' on textualization: Burnshaw and Peyre

Work on the French section with Henri Peyre began at the same time as the German section in December 1958 but continued beyond it to the end of 1959. Burnshaw's correspondence with Peyre drew on the experience of the fraught exchanges with his German contributors. He confided that 'with Hugo and the other Germans' he had needed to revise 'pieces to the extent of a total rewriting' (Burnshaw, 1959d). Burnshaw also had substantial direct involvement with the French section. Peyre was not only the associate editor for French but also the principal contributor, providing translations and commentaries for 11 of the 13 poets included in his section. Burnshaw then acted as his editor in a practice that was distinct from the Spanish and Italian sections, where most of the work took place between associate editors Dudley Fitts and John Frederick Nims and their Spanish or Portuguese and Italian contributors respectively.

Peyre's detailed response to the Mallarmé specimen established an active role for him in the conception and formulation of the project, involving him in early rituals of recognition. Unlike Hugo and the other German contributors, he had already begun to form a collaborative working relationship with Burnshaw before the editing of his own contributions. Peyre was effusive in his praise of Burnshaw, describing him as a 'martyr of poetry' (Peyre, 1959c), and was also willing to play a compliant role, confiding that he would expect a 'scolding' from Burnshaw's editing (Peyre, 1959b). Burnshaw reciprocated the admiration, responding to an early sample of Peyre's contributions that he was 'delighted': 'I can tell you my reaction in a word: Magnifique' (Burnshaw, 1959d).

After the unresolved conflicts and compromises of the German section, Burnshaw was still working out the collaborative method of *The Poem Itself*, instructing Peyre that 'by far the best procedure' was 'for you to do a few sample "attacks" on the problem and for me to react to these, and then for you to consider my reactions and then to do the whole job as you see best' (Burnshaw, 1959j). In spite of Peyre's earlier involvement in the proposal and specimen, Burnshaw felt the need to set out the translation principles of the anthology again, referring back to his experience with the German section. 'I have been insisting on literalness,' he declared, although some contributors had 'found this a hard line to hew to', slipping into '"poetical literal renderings"', requiring a firm reminder from Burnshaw of the 'basic plan' of the anthology (Burnshaw, 1959j). He represented the ensuing exchanges as follows:

> **But then they have said, in effect, that there is no literal way of saying what such-and-such a word or phrase means; and I have said in reply: 'Indeed there isn't always a satisfactory equivalent, and that is why we have been resorting to interpolated words and phrases or even sentences.'** (Burnshaw, 1959j)

This is a curious revision of the actual exchanges that Burnshaw had with his German contributors. His correspondence with Sebba shows conflict arising not from contributors slipping into 'poetical renderings' but from Burnshaw pushing his own interpretations and word choices, irrespective of a range of semantic considerations. Burnshaw's revisionary dramatization of these exchanges side-stepped his substantial conflicts with the German contributors, attempting to return to the terms on which he had first proposed the project to Peyre and Fitts as a correction to a prevailing culture of poetic '"recreations"' (Burnshaw, 1958a). It is less an account of his experience than a retreat to the initial conceptualization of the project before it came into contact with challenges to his method.

Peyre responded with an effective blend of compliance and resistance to Burnshaw's proposition. He was willing to go along with the polemical impetus of Burnshaw's objection to poetic recreation, assuring him that he wished to 'avoid high flown, personal vision' and 'falsely poetical' work (Peyre, 1959a). However, he was also able to challenge the practices that Burnshaw had established in the German section. When Burnshaw suggested using interpolations in brackets as he had done with the German contributors (Burnshaw, 1959d), Peyre set out his objection. While he felt that 'all your contributors should bow' to 'the policy of literalness', he maintained that 'literalness may not mean fidelity and to be excessively prosaic is as much of a betrayal as to be poetical' (Burnshaw's underlining). In the case of a poet who 'is primarily a musician like Verlaine', he felt an exception could be 'tolerated' (Peyre, 1959c). In a further letter, he declared, 'my one plea to you is: in a very, very few cases, I believe the musical element of the poetry should be stressed in the commentary, and be conveyed in the translation' (Peyre's underlining), citing Baudelaire's 'L'Invitation au voyage' and Verlaine's 'Bruxelles'. In these cases, 'we might make a slight exception of literalness (which would be prosaism) and render the musical value of the poem' (Peyre, 1959d).

Burnshaw referred repeatedly to keeping 'our promise to the reader' as a justification for his 'truly literal' translation method (Burnshaw, 1959j). His discussions with Sebba turned primarily on the semantic implication of German words and phrases rather than the reader's experience of the translations. This approach led to translations that made considerable syntactic demands on the reader. Peyre adopted Burnshaw's conceptual focus on the reader and then used it to challenge the use of brackets: 'On the rather lavish use of alternate renderings and square brackets which you recommend, I would also formulate timid doubts', elaborating that 'it can take up much space, slow down the reading, sound heavily didactic. It underlines too crudely the possible ambiguities of the text' (Burnshaw's underlining) (Peyre, 1959c).

Where Burnshaw had continued to advocate for his method and his translation choices with his German contributors, he conceded willingly to Peyre's objections:

> I've thought about all the points you raise and I agree with them completely, and especially with your reservations about some of my suggestions and proposals. It would be sorry indeed if my principle of literalness were to compel our contributors to become excessively prosaic. (Burnshaw, 1959k)

He now concluded that 'alternate renderings in square brackets and parentheses can surely be horrible if overused' (Burnshaw, 1959k). Brackets are almost entirely absent from Baudelaire's 'Le Balcon' and the poems by Verlaine, and generally used more sparingly in the French section.

Peyre prompted Burnshaw to a more open, responsive reflection on his advocacy for the project. He confessed that he was 'learning much about the method in the course of all this editing' (Burnshaw, 1959m) and exclaimed at one point, 'How dreary it would be if everyone followed that Mallarmé specimen!' (Burnshaw, 1959l). His exchanges with Peyre also paid greater attention to what he described as the 'interpretative-explanatory-helpful commentary' (Burnshaw, 1959j). His editing of the German section had concentrated primarily on the translations. Burnshaw made a common criticism throughout the anthology that the commentaries failed to address formal properties and the 'poem qua poem' (Burnshaw, 1959e). Peyre, by contrast, had done 'admirably in pointing to the poetical qualities and in helping him [the reader] to understand the sense of the poem' (Burnshaw, 1959j).

One can see this more harmonious collaboration between editor and contributor in Burnshaw's close involvement with the further Mallarmé contributions. After editing Peyre's translations and commentaries, he wrote to say that he had 'indulged' his interest in the poems, 'adding and changing with great audacity' (Burnshaw, 1959m). Burnshaw 'entirely retyped' the typescripts of these contributions, so it is hard to ascertain with precision where he intervened (Burnshaw, 1959m). The correspondence presents no evidence of conflict. Burnshaw praised Peyre's Mallarmé commentaries as 'a perfect example of our method at its most effective' and 'extremely well discussed in terms of [...] poetic effects' (Burnshaw, 1959m). For his part, Peyre thought that Burnshaw's editing of these contributions was 'excellent', declaring that he had 'greatly improved, clarified, strengthened what I had meant to say' (Peyre, 1959e).

Mallarmé's 'Le vierge, le vivace, y le bel aujourd'hui' provides an example of a translation and commentary that realized Burnshaw's advocacy at the level of method and personal interpretation to both his and his contributor's apparent satisfaction. It can therefore be assessed as a point where his initial conceptual proposal to address both the syntax and the sound of the poem reached a stable agreement as collaborative practice, akin to Farrell's stage of 'instrumental intimacy' where the cognitive processes of participants can merge (2001, p. 23). The commentary describes the poem as 'an image of mystifying intent' (Burnshaw, 1964, p. 54), an interpretative challenge. The interpretative comment is interspersed with a translation that is broken down into sections. The opening of the poem is presented thus:

> Le vierge, le vivace et le bel aujourd'hui
> Va-t-il nous déchirer avec un coup d'aile ivre
> Ce lac dur oublié que hante sous le givre
> Le transparent glacier des vols qui n'ont pas fui!
>
> ...
>
> The first stanza is both an exclamation and a question. It seizes us by the surprise of the three resplendent adjectives of the opening line, and when we come upon the *nous* of the second, we are directly involved. (1) *The virgin, the vivid and the splendid new day* – this new day bristling with life – (2) *Will it tear for us with a stroke of its drunken wing* (3) *This hard forgotten lake haunted beneath the frost* (4) *By the transparent glacier of flights that have not fled!* (Burnshaw, 1964, p. 54)

Burnshaw wrote to Peyre to say that in his editing he had placed 'the interpretation closer to the literal translation' (Burnshaw, 1959m), a practice that had worked elsewhere in the anthology, although Peyre himself had earlier suggested this practice 'to prepare the reader for the translation coming next' (Peyre,

1959d). The commentary provides an interpretative framework for the translation rather than a supplement to it. In the initial conception of the project, the commentary had a secondary status with Peyre's suggestions for 'Don du poème' appended as an afterthought. Here the commentary guides the reader towards particular aspects of the opening stanza, such as syntactic ambiguity (a period that is both exclamation and question), grammatical form (use of adjectives), and the experience and position of the reader ('surprise' and the use of *nous*). The figurative interpretation of the opening line ('this new day bristling with life') further integrates the guiding voice of the commentary with the experience of reading the translation. It directs the reader and leaves them with less work than the cluttered practice of brackets that Burnshaw pushed with the German contributions. Although this is a dense poem, the arrangement of translation and commentary provides a more legible and more coherent reading experience than the entries for Hofmannsthal and Rilke that I discussed earlier. One consequence of this greater coherence is that the link to the source text is weakened. Where, at least in theory, *The Poem Itself* proposed that the reader should integrate the matter of the translation and commentary in a reading of the source text of the poem, here the reader can gain a reasonably integrated experience by moving between translation and commentary independently of the source. Clive Scott argues that, in spite of the claims of much prose translation, as a form it cannot avoid a degree of ontological independence from the source text. This arrangement of translation and commentary creates a form of ontological independence for the reading experience in English.

One can see that in this entry Burnshaw and Peyre maintain the focus of Burnshaw's initial proposal on syntax and sound. Burnshaw stated that 'the syntax cannot fail to discourage even a hardy reader' as he edited Peyre's Mallarmé contributions (Burnshaw, 1959m). Syntax is a well-established focus of the critical literature on Mallarmé. For Jacques Derrida, the interpretative challenge of his poems, their 'undecidability', derives not so much from 'the richness of meaning, the inexhaustible resources of a word', but from 'a certain play of the syntax', citing a notorious comment that was attributed to Mallarmé, '"I am profoundly and scrupulously a syntaxer"' (1992, p. 114).

Malcolm Bowie (1978, pp. 10-11) notes two remarkable syntactic features in the passage I have cited above. The grammatical status of *vierge* and *vivace* is ambiguous: they can be read initially as nouns, as 'phantom presences' that are resolved as adjectives qualifying *aujourd'hui* as the line unfolds. The pronoun *nous* could also be read as a direct or indirect object, thus either *ce lac* (this lake) or the reader could be torn by the drunken wing. As I noted earlier, the Peyre–Burnshaw entry is conscious of syntax. Where Hartley's translation of the opening line ('The virginal, living and beautiful day', p. 85) chooses the clearly adjectival 'virginal' and 'living', *The Poem Itself* offers the more ambiguous 'The virgin, the vivid...'. Yet the ambiguity is mitigated by the commentary, which pre-empts the syntax in this case with reference to 'the three resplendent adjectives'. While the commentary notes the way that *nous* involves the reader, the translation chooses to explicate the indirect object, thus removing the reader from the violent implication of *déchirer* (to tear).

The coherence and interpretative efficiency of the commentary and translation mitigate the disruptive effects of syntactic ambiguity in Mallarmé's poem. In his own commentary on 'Le vierge, le vivace . . .', Bowie notes that the difficulty of the poem provokes readers to adopt different forms of 'defensive reaction': to 'make it into a picture' and to 'superimpose upon the picture a simple allegorical grid' (1978, p. 10), the swan as the poet and so on. The poem is thus 'tidied up' and 'rigidified' (1978, p. 10). One can see these tendencies in the ways that the Burnshaw–Peyre commentary deals not only with syntax but also with sound, one of the primary concerns of Burnshaw's initial proposal for the anthology. For Bowie, the poem's 'arresting and intricate' pattern of sounds resists interpretation; it is liable to attract a reader's attention before they seek 'to acquire anything more than a minimum supporting drift of sense' (1978, p. 10). Clive Scott refers to this mnemonic aspect of poetry as ensuring 'the survival of a text in its non-interpreted, or pre-interpreted, integrity' (2000, p. 153). *The Poem Itself* consistently attempts to interpret this element of the poem, explaining it, in one of Bowie's 'defensive gestures', as confirmation of the poem's setting, its 'picture': the sound *i* or *ui* 'has something of the angular sharpness of ice itself'; lines 'begin to tighten in an ice-like gloom'; and 'longer words, with an accumulation of *i*'s', produce 'an impression of vast, desolate plains of ice' (Burnshaw, 1964, p. 55). The initial proposal for *The Poem Itself* aimed to deliver the reader to the source text so that they could experience, among other things, the sounds of poems in foreign languages. The commentary here relates sound directly to referential meaning, making sense of it but, as with the poem's syntax, leaving the reader scant leeway to make their own sense of the movement from reading experience to interpretation.

The Peyre–Burnshaw commentary does provide the caveat that its interpretation is partial, enjoining 'the interested reader who may prefer a different reading to ours' to remember Robert Frost's statement that '"a poet is entitled to all the meanings that can be found in his poem"' (Burnshaw, 1964, p. 54). Although its approach conforms to the 'defensive mechanisms' that Bowie notes – a reliance on setting and allegory – it nevertheless brings out a range of ways of conceiving the swan – as a symbol of 'unattainable perfection', of 'vigor', a 'pure, solitary ideal', a 'proud dream' and a 'martyr' (Burnshaw, 1964, pp. 54, 55). The poem solicits these approaches even as it disrupts them and there is only so much that can be said in a two-page spread. Yet an approach that would be attentive to the experience of the poem needs to account for aspects of the reading experience that either resist interpretation (as in the case of sound for Bowie and Scott) or challenge it. Bowie describes Mallarmé's poetry as a 'sense-making system' (1978, p. 12). Burnshaw claimed in similar terms as he edited the commentary for 'Le vierge, le vivace . . .', that he had 'called attention to the sort of meaning-search that goes on nowadays' (1959m). However, the impulse to clarify and explain frequently overrode that experience of reading and sense-making.

Reflecting on literal translation practices at the time of Burnshaw's anthology, Daniel Weissbort describes *The Poem Itself* approvingly as 'useful', if nevertheless dependent on 'an unavoidably elaborate apparatus' (2010, p. 115). The degree of elaborateness and difficulty varies considerably from one section and from one contribution to another. The archive gives access to the social and cultural factors that led to these varied manifestations of Burnshaw's advocacy. Some of the most elaborate, and demanding, translation occurs in the German section where Burnshaw was still working out his method. This stage of the project was characterized by the least stable executive and personal social relations, where trust was scarce on both sides. The reader is left to manage as best they can with translations that bear the trace of antagonistic readings of the poems' semantic implication. Burnshaw's advocacy for a method of translation was here overtaken by advocacy for his own interpretation of the poems. This move was masked in his revisionary account of these exchanges to Henri Peyre, which attempted to return to the initial conceptualization of the project. Peyre's ability to combine emollience with firm resistance, and his more openly collaborative relationship with Burnshaw, led to a more legible translation practice and coherent reading experience across translation and commentary, albeit one whose interpretative efficiency could be pre-emptive. Burnshaw drove his advocacy under the banner of a 'truly literal' translation. His editorial exchanges show not only how textually diverse the concept can be in terms of practice but also how that diversity answered to particular working relations with different contributors. A genetic approach to the creation of *The Poem Itself* enables an understanding of Burnshaw's advocacy as a succession of encounters between conceptual proposition and textual practice, which were animated and shaped by varied social interactions. A highly ambitious enterprise and a substantial work of labour, the published text can be read as both the result and the articulation of that collaborative process of persuasion, disagreement, negotiation and compromise.

References

Bellemin-Noël, J. (1977) Reproduir le manuscrit, présenter les brouillons, établir un avant-texte. *Littérature*, 28, 3–18.

de Biasi, P.-M. (1996) What is a literary draft? Toward a functional typology of genetic documentation. Trans. I. Wassenaar, *Yale French Studies*, 89, 26–58.

— (2004) Toward a science of literature: Manuscript analysis and the genesis of the work, in Deppman, J., Ferrer, D. and Groden, M. (eds), *Genetic Criticism: Texts and avant-textes*. Philadelphia, PN: University of Pennsylvania Press, pp. 36–68.

Bowie, M. (1978) *Mallarmé and the Art of Being Difficult*. Cambridge: Cambridge University Press.

Burnshaw, S. (1958a) Letter to Harry Levin, 13 February 1958. Stanley Burnshaw Papers, Box 5/Folder 6, Harry Ransom Center, The University of Texas at Austin.

— (1958b) Letter to Dudley Fitts, 14 February 1958. Stanley Burnshaw Papers, 5/6, Harry Ransom Center, The University of Texas at Austin.

— (1958c) Letter to Henri Peyre, 7 October 1958. Stanley Burnshaw Papers, 5/6, Harry Ransom Center, The University of Texas at Austin.

— (1959a) Letter to Dudley Fitts, 6 January 1959. Stanley Burnshaw Papers, 4/6, Harry Ransom Center, The University of Texas at Austin.

— (1959b) Letter to Howard Hugo, 2 June 1959. Stanley Burnshaw Papers, 4/10, Harry Ransom Center, The University of Texas at Austin.

— (1959c) Letter to Howard Hugo, 4 June 1959. Stanley Burnshaw Papers, 4/10, Harry Ransom Center, The University of Texas at Austin.

— (1959d) Letter to Henri Peyre, 1 July 1959. Stanley Burnshaw Papers, 5/3, Harry Ransom Center, The University of Texas at Austin.

— (1959e) Letter to Dudley Fitts, 4 July 1959. Stanley Burnshaw Papers, 4/7, Harry Ransom Center, The University of Texas at Austin.

— (1959f) Letter to Gregor Sebba, 10 July 1959. Stanley Burnshaw Papers, 4/12, Harry Ransom Center, The University of Texas at Austin.

— (1959g) Typescript, c. 10 July 1959. Stanley Burnshaw Papers, 4/12, Harry Ransom Center, The University of Texas at Austin.

— (1959h) Letter to Howard Hugo, 11 July 1959. Stanley Burnshaw Papers, 4/11, Harry Ransom Center, The University of Texas at Austin.

— (1959i) Letter to Gregor Sebba, 16 July 1959. Stanley Burnshaw Papers, 4/12, Harry Ransom Center, The University of Texas at Austin.

— (1959j) Letter to Henri Peyre, 17 July 1959. Stanley Burnshaw Papers, 5/3, Harry Ransom Center, The University of Texas at Austin.

— (1959k) Letter to Henri Peyre, 21 September 1959. Stanley Burnshaw Papers, 5/3, Harry Ransom Center, The University of Texas at Austin.

— (1959l) Letter to Henri Peyre, 26 September 1959. Stanley Burnshaw Papers, 5/3, Harry Ransom Center, The University of Texas at Austin.

— (1959m) Letter to Henri Peyre, 8 December 1959. Stanley Burnshaw Papers, 5/3, Harry Ransom Center, The University of Texas at Austin.

— (1964) *The Poem Itself: 150 European poems translated and analysed*. Harmondsworth: Penguin.

— (n.d.i) Proposal, n.d. Stanley Burnshaw Papers, 5/6, Harry Ransom Center, The University of Texas at Austin.

— (n.d.ii) Typescript, n.d. Stanley Burnshaw Papers, 5/6, Harry Ransom Center, The University of Texas at Austin.

— (n.d.iii) Typescript, n.d. Stanley Burnshaw Papers, 5/6, Harry Ransom Center, The University of Texas at Austin.

— (n.d.iv) Letter to Andrew O. Jaszi, n.d. Stanley Burnshaw Papers, 4/11, Harry Ransom Center, The University of Texas at Austin.

Catford, J. C. (1965) *A Linguistic Theory of Translation: An essay in applied linguistics*. London: Oxford University Press.

Chesterman, A. (2017) *Reflections on Translation Theory: Selected papers 1993–2014*. Amsterdam: John Benjamins.

Cohen, J. M. (ed), (1958) *The Penguin Book of Italian Verse*. Harmondsworth: Penguin.

Cordingley, A. (2020) Genetic Criticism, in Baker, M. and Saldanha, G. (eds), *Routledge Encyclopedia of Translation Studies*. London: Routledge, pp. 208–13.

— and Frigau Manning, C. (eds) (2017) *Collaborative Translation: From the Renaissance to the Digital Age*. London: Bloomsbury.

Debray Genette, R. (1979) Génétique et poétique: le cas de Flaubert, in *Essais de critique génétique*. Paris: Flammarion, pp. 21–67.

Derrida, J. (1992) *Mallarmé*. Trans. Roulston, C., in Attridge, D. (ed), *Acts of Literature*. London: Routledge, pp. 110–26.

Dimitrova, B. E. (2005) *Expertise and Explicitation in the Translation Process*. Amsterdam: John Benjamins.

Farrell, M. P. (2001) *Collaborative Circles: Friendship dynamics and creative work*. Chicago, IL: University of Chicago Press.

Ferrer, D. (2011) *Logiques du brouillon: Modèles pour une critique génétique*. Paris: Seuil.

Fitts, D. (1942) *An Anthology of Contemporary Latin American Poetry*, Norfolk, CT: New Directions.

— (1958a) Letter to Stanley Burnshaw, 16 February 1958. Stanley Burnshaw Papers, 5/6, Harry Ransom Center, The University of Texas at Austin.

— (1958b) Letter to Stanley Burnshaw, 21 November 1958. Stanley Burnshaw Papers, 5/6, Harry Ransom Center, The University of Texas at Austin.

Fowlie, W. (1953) *Mallarmé*. London: Dennis Dobson.

Hartley, A. (1965) *The Penguin Book of French Verse 3: The nineteenth century*. Harmondsworth: Penguin.

Hölderlin, F. (1961) *Selected Verse*. Translated and introduced by Hamburger, M. Harmondsworth: Penguin, 1961.

Jaszi, A. O. (n. d.) Typeset n.d. Stanley Burnshaw Papers, 4/11, Harry Ransom Center, The University of Texas at Austin.

Levin, H. (1958) Letter to Stanley Burnshaw, 19 February 1958.

Stanley Burnshaw Papers, 5/6, Harry Ransom Center, The University of Texas at Austin.

Peyre, H. (1958a) Letter to Stanley Burnshaw, 15 October 1958. Stanley Burnshaw Papers, 5/6, Harry Ransom Center, The University of Texas at Austin.

— (1958b) Letter to Stanley Burnshaw, 24 October 1958. Stanley Burnshaw Papers, 5/6, Harry Ransom Center, The University of Texas at Austin.

— (1959a) Letter to Stanley Burnshaw, 20 April 1959. Stanley Burnshaw Papers, 5/3, Harry Ransom Center, The University of Texas at Austin.

— (1959b) Letter to Stanley Burnshaw, 9 July 1959. Stanley Burnshaw Papers, 5/3, Harry Ransom Center, The University of Texas at Austin.

— (1959c) Letter to Stanley Burnshaw, 14 September 1959. Stanley Burnshaw Papers, 5/3, Harry Ransom Center, The University of Texas at Austin.

— (1959d) Letter to Stanley Burnshaw, 25 September 1959. Stanley Burnshaw Papers, 5/3, Harry Ransom Center, The University of Texas at Austin.

— (1959e) Letter to Stanley Burnshaw, 11 December 1959. Stanley Burnshaw Papers, 7/6, Harry Ransom Center, The University of Texas.

Robinson, D. (1998) Literal translation, in Baker, M. (ed), *Routledge Encyclopedia of Translation Studies*. London: Routledge, pp. 125–7.

Scott, C. (2000) *Translating Baudelaire*. Exeter: University of Exeter Press.

Sebba, G. (1959) Letter to Stanley Burnshaw, 14 July 1959. Stanley Burnshaw Papers, 4/12, Harry Ransom Center, The University of Texas at Austin.

— (n.d.) Letter to Stanley Burnshaw, n.d. Stanley Burnshaw Papers, 4/12, Harry Ransom Center, The University of Texas at Austin.

Shuttleworth, M. and Cowie, M. (2014) *Dictionary of Translation Studies*. London and New York: Routledge.

Steiner, G. (1992) *After Babel: Aspects of language and translation*, 2nd edn. Oxford: Oxford University Press.

Trilling, L. (1984) The Poem Itself. *Agenda, Stanley Burnshaw Special Issue*, 21 (4)–22 (1), 95–8.

Weissbort, D. (2010) Ted Hughes and the translatable. *Comparative Critical Studies*, 7 (1), 107–19.

Wimsatt, W. K. and Beardsley, M. C. (1954) *The Verbal Icon: Studies in the meaning of poetry*. Lexington, KY: University of Kentucky Press.

5

Advocacy and recognition: S. I. Hsiung, a translator of the Chinese diaspora

Lisha Xu

Overview

This chapter examines advocacy and recognition as two central concerns of translation. It does so through reference to the work of S. I. Hsiung, a key writer and translator of the Chinese diaspora of the early decades of the twentieth century. This was a time of extraordinary debate in China, when many sought to present a more modern image of the nation in an increasingly fractious geopolitical situation, not only through questioning the conditions of representation and reception of Chinese writing in the context of the colonial anglophone West but also through rethinking the potential of translation itself to promote the conditions of a more equitable cultural encounter. In this context, diasporic writers like Hsiung turned to translation as a mode of advocacy that had the capacity to function both as a direct antidote to colonial misrecognition and, culturally, ideologically and racially, as the source of a new hermeneutic trust.

Introduction

Salman Rushdie's 'Having been borne across the world, we are translated men' (1992, p. 17) is more than an acknowledgement of the inevitability of personal and cultural adjustment in the wake of migrancy. His essay *Imaginary Homelands* also recognizes the psychological journeying of the migrant, between the sense of loss implicit in displacement and the possibility of advancement offered by the new context. The idea of translation, in this way, refers to the complex interaction between loss and gain not solely in terms of what happens to text but also as a competing tension within the individual life when the sense of psychological security implicit in belonging, in the idea of homeland, is deracinated and forced to graft onto the living tissue of unfamiliar worlds. But, while it evokes the disruption inherent in border-crossing, translation, for Rushdie, also offers the possibility of a central act of self-construction, a creative encounter with the new. Willingly or unwillingly, diasporic writers like Rushdie, who travel between worlds, are 'translated' because their life and writing are shaped by their migrant experience, by the inevitably zigzag trajectory between the familiar and the unfamiliar, prompting respectively what is frequently an abiding sense of loss and the anxieties of acceptance and belonging.

In his *The Location of Culture*, Homi Bhabha similarly identifies the translational identity of those who cross borders as one of flux, of a fluidity of being: 'We find ourselves in the moment of transit where space and time cross to produce complex figures of difference and identity, past and present, inside and outside, inclusion and exclusion' (1994, p. 1). Taken in these terms, diasporic experience inevitably opens up the possibility of what we might think of as a translational consciousness, not in the sense merely of the processes of contrast and comparison inherent to transit but as a response – painful, wary, creative or excited – to a new context experienced through hybridity, shifting ambivalences and plural identities that are all more instantly perceptible than in the life left behind. In this way, much diasporic writing becomes an act of translation of the writer's migrant experience, of their already translational encounter between realities fixed and unfixed, of the remembrance of and the nostalgia for whatever is meant by 'home'. This chapter asks how this experience of displacement, geographical and psychological, translates the writer into writer-translator. In other words, how might the writing of translation be underpinned by the search to fashion a new home out of this state of flux, of betweenness, and, in particular, how can it function as a space of advocacy for the sort of encounter where a new quality of belonging is forged, a space where the translator presents old worlds meaningfully to the new?

In order to address these central questions, this chapter examines the experience of key Chinese writer and translator S. I. Hsiung (1902–91), who migrated from China to Britain in 1932 and whose work – essay, fiction and translation alike – is infused with the experience of transit and the complex interplays of exclusion and inclusion that transit gives rise to. In this way, all of his work is translational (even the work he produced when he returned to China, for he saw it then through different eyes), writing as he does from the centre of his experience as a migrant where translation is both an inevitable feature of everyday life and a key method for advocating across dislocated and deeply felt otherness to the apparently securely located self.

By the time Hsiung joined what was already the centuries-old Chinese diaspora, he was steadily acquiring in both Beijing and Shanghai the reputation of a jobbing translator (of texts as varied as *The Autobiography of Benjamin Franklin* in 1929 and plays by J. M. Barrie, including *The Admirable Crichton* in 1930 and *Peter Pan* in 1931). In the social and political ferment of the China of the time, every act of translation was considered an important salvo in the crucial battle to open up the country to what the followers of the New Culture Movement argued were the modernizing currents of the West, so that translation for Hsiung was already infused with a sense of, at the very least, its cultural utility. But in his new home city of London, where he soon settled, he was quickly to bring this sense of the cultural work of translation to an extraordinary level, becoming the first Chinese translator to present Peking Opera (京剧) – the best known of the many hugely complex classical Chinese operatic forms – on the professional London stage. There continues to be a strong modernist and modernizing tone to his work, but now directionality has been reversed and in his representation of classical Chinese cultures he sought deliberately to offer to the world map the image of a China radically different from imagined ancient Cathay (Hsiung in Zheng, 2015, p. 289). As a translator displaced at this seminal moment in the history of the rising modern China and turning to the estranging but – by the proponents of the New Culture Movement at least – also much-admired West, Hsiung in his life and in his work inevitably resisted and rethought the dominant representation and reception of China. Now a translated man himself, subject to the interplay of exclusion and inclusion in his own life, as we shall see, the translator crucially moves to address the assumptions of Sino-Western cultural exchange which radically othered the Chinese-speaking world, culturally, ideologically and racially. As a counter to the migrant's fear of misrecognition and the pain of racism, Hsiung turns to translating as both embodiment and projection of the mobile and fluid identity that is emerging from the instability and fragmentation of his border-crossing self. In this way, translation itself becomes a vehicle of advocacy for a recognition of self and origins alike, meaningful now in its aim to ignite hermeneutic engagement within the receiving context without allowing that context to completely assimilate the complex of differences that characterize the sources of the self and the culture that originally gave it contextual meaning. Hsiung, a convinced supporter of the reforming aims of the New Culture Movement, naturally saw himself as a Chinese modern whose country was emerging as a liberal society from the stranglehold of its feudal past, so that by retranslating China he was also effectively retranslating himself, presenting his own credentials as a modern citizen. In its offer of the possibility of connection as an antidote to the exclusion that is implicit in the act of othering, Hsiung begins to understand translation not simply as a method of cultural transmission and enrichment China-inwards, but now, in his need to engineer new conditions of belonging, he resorts to it as a solution to (re)wiring the two worlds and, at the same time, as a medium of resistance to the Anglosphere's routine exoticization of the Chinese-speaking world. For this precursor of the cultural and ethical turns in Translation Studies, translation necessarily becomes a cultural practice that, by promoting the conditions of encounter between both worlds, might serve as a source of more equitable recognition.

The translated translator

As both a self-conscious modern and Anglophile, Hsiung was eager to fit in and feel accepted by his new home. In the first phase of his new life, at least, the external markers of his integration were those of any migrant, woven indelibly into the quality of his social and cultural communication with the new homeplace. But as a translator, who anxiously scrutinized the end product of process, he was painfully aware of how decontextualization may all too often cause that product to be viewed as pastiche. His sense of cultural uprooting, allied to the constant assessment of his own performance as acceptable 'other', produced what we might think of as a crisis of perceived reception, an impostor syndrome arising from the anxiety as to whether these external markers of his acceptance were empty acts of ventriloquism (see, for example, Hawley, 2019, p. 203).

Of course, Hsiung had set the bar of acceptance high. The major external markers of his performance, in his view, included not only English proficiency – which in his case was of exceptional standard – but also recognition as a man of letters from the elite literary circles of the capital. Soon after his arrival in London, Hsiung began contacting writers such as George Bernard Shaw, J. M. Barrie, John Galsworthy and John Drinkwater to ask them to read his English-language writings, in search of the acceptance that he himself deemed the 'greatest ambition' of his new status (Hsiung, 1946, p. 194). Using his earlier translations of their work into Chinese as his networking capital, Hsiung sent them the manuscript of his recent English translation of his own play *Mammon* (财神, 1935). Both Barrie and Drinkwater wrote praising his English-language proficiency as a second-language user, which piqued Hsiung's deeply rooted sense of ontological anxiety when he worried that '[Barrie and Drinkwater] are just trying to be polite to me' (Hsiung, 2010, p. 29, my translation). Meanwhile, the more characteristically barbed Shaw commented that Hsiung's English was 'Chinese English, which is better than that of many English people' (Hsiung, 2010, p. 29, my translation) so that even more than half a century later, Hsiung still recalled his anguish when mulling over Shaw's comments: 'Shaw's comments are elusive. Sarcasm? [...] I thought about [...] stopping writing in English, in case I embarrassed myself' (Hsiung, 2010, p. 29, my translation). This corrosive fear of ridicule, however, was rapidly exacerbated by what he interpreted as an act of exclusion from the golden circle of literary studies. Immediately upon arriving in London, Hsiung sent a carefully crafted PhD proposal on Shakespeare to his chosen supervisor, Allardyce Nicoll, only to receive the reply: 'Mr. Hsiung... You can't compete with what English students have to say about Shakespeare, no matter how good your English is' (Hsiung, 2010, p. 26, my translation). The 'impostor' in Hsiung anguished that Shakespeare's Englishness made of the writer a closed book, his thought and art constrained within a hermeneutic circle closed off to any outsider. Nicoll's words of counsel were kindly meant, reflecting a nationalism in some strands of Shakespearean studies that Gary Taylor effectively felt constrained to contest in his *Reinventing Shakespeare: A Cultural History from the Restoration to the Present* (1991), published more than half a century later (see, especially, pp. 121–4). It was a formative incident, feeding into Hsiung's anxiety of exclusion but also sharpening his desire to belong, underlining to him the importance of mediating his Chinese background into the assumptions of his seemingly (in the translational sense) inhospitable hosts. The barrier was of course linguistic, but only on the surface, so that in the presence of a cultural gatekeeper like Nicoll, Hsiung immediately felt the force of an exclusion that was racially based, although couched in epistemological terms.

At the core of Nicoll's rejection was a cultural exceptionalism that not only attached to the perceived position of Shakespeare as national dramatist but also disallowed the potential validity of translation itself. In this view, the translated man was necessarily an impostor, and the product of translation as inevitably nothing more than a deficient simulacrum of the original.

Hsiung's focus, however, was no longer on translation *into* but translation *between*. The theatre presented itself to him not only as a space where the impostor might study the social and political contours of a society but also as a medium for the complex interactions of representation that the translated translator might seek to deploy in his search for mutual understanding. In his late-published memoir, Hsiung credited 'the audiences from theatres in London' as his 'best supervisors' in this dual objective:

> **During my translation, I went to see almost every play in London theatres, no matter the play is a failure or a success. I observed how the audiences react to what happened on stage. The audience's reaction to the stage is where I benefited the most.** (Hsiung, 2010, p. 30, my translation)

By observing spectators' reactions, Hsiung began to think about how he might perform his own background on the London stage and what kind of creative interventions in his translation might create the conditions of the shared understanding that was the key marker of his acceptance. The impostor reminds the translator to be ever mindful of the need to engage the London audience by negotiating the perceived gaps between the local theatre context and the conventions of Peking Opera, which he had chosen as the most appropriate vehicle for the complex translational project that would give form to the flux of his experience and his desire for shared understanding alike.

The early 1930s had witnessed an upsurge of interest in Peking Opera in the West, as acclaimed star performer Mei Lanfang and his company toured in the United States, in Mei's own words as a 'cultural ambassador' (quoted in Qi, 2015, p. 164), so that, effectively, the form's accrued status as national theatre within China was harnessed by Mei as a key selling point for his American performances. For Mei, Chinese opera (*xiqu*) coalesces around a complex set of vocal and physical performance codes (see, for example, Qi, 2005). This is of course true of both opera and classical ballet in the West, although in both cases their appeal is much more socially prescribed. The dramatic, operatic and balletic codes that animate *xiqu*, however, are inherited and distilled from ancient Chinese folk and philosophical sources, so that even a relatively more recent form like Peking Opera, whose elaborate staging complexities had been honed in the late eighteenth-century court in the Forbidden City, still enjoys widespread popularity. Hsiung himself had grown up listening to Peking Opera (Hsiung, 2010) and chose to translate one of its best-known pieces – *Lady Precious Stream*[1] – not because of an insurmountable attachment to home, nor out of an adherence to the 'nationalistic message' that inheres in many ways to the form today (Goldstein, 2007, p. 178; Xu and Johnston, 2022, p. 325), but rather to advocate for the complexity of his own position as a Chinese migrant in London in the 1930s. Moreover, if Shakespeare was deemed fully intelligible only within the golden circle of a particular linguistic and cultural understanding, then this particular translation project was designed to show that such commodification was merely a failure to understand translation and the dynamics of understanding that it might trigger. Hsiung deliberately chose to translate a play that not only represented the best of a living tradition of Chinese performance art but also might just as easily be deemed as untranslatable as Shakespeare if considered in terms of its embodiment of perceived national essence.

---

[1] *Lady Precious Stream* is Hsiung's English translation of *Wang Baochuan* (王宝钏), a story that originates in early nineteenth-century folk lyrics and one of the most popular Peking Operas performed in the early twentieth century. The original performance Hsiung chose for the basis of his translation of *Lady Precious Stream* was the 'Eight Excerpts about the Wang Family' (1949, p. xvi), which are now seldom performed as a whole play but instead appear as independent excerpts within other plays. The stage production of this play opened on 27 November 1934 at The Little Theatre in London (the theatre was destroyed during the London Blitz) and ran for an astonishing 900 nights before touring to other cities such as Dublin, Shanghai and New York.

Painfully aware of his own betweenness, Hsiung was anxious to create something that would facilitate understanding and engineer connection. In psychological terms, both theatre as play-acting and translation as encounter allowed him to create a hyperreal world where he could be both impostor and accepted. The parameters of his specific project are cultural, but for the migrant are equally real in existential terms. And in both cases, everyday life and the stage, the project entails a leap of faith, a huge risk for both migrant and translator alike, in that within the act of translation conceived in this way, there is the movement away from one natural state into a state whose parameters of so-called naturalness can be questioned. The 'translated man' internalizes the sense of being deracinated and denaturalized, forced to perform in an environment in which he – Hsiung – can never be sure that his performance is considered authentic by others within that group. This sense of being denatured is perhaps intrinsic to the scrutiny that the dislocated self brings to bear on the performing self, and as Hsiung transited relentlessly between both positions he began to regard source conditions and target aspirations alike as incompatible – an abiding anxiety of irreconcilability that surely still bedevils many translation projects.

At times, this presents a sense of painful critique of Chinese culture. In an introductory article published to sensitize his London audience to the basic conventions of *xiqu* staging, he mocks Peking Opera's performance codes as 'even more ridiculous' (1934, p. 3) than anything the spectator might conjure from the dominant discourse of chinoiserie. Such self-deprecation, on the one hand, indicates the translator's anxiety to create the conditions of difference by which his play might work on stage. On the other, the translated translator, through his entertaining reassurance to the in-group audience that he acknowledges their cultural positions, is no less cautiously advocating for his own position as a writer caught in between, responsive to the gap between Peking Opera performance codes and London spectators' potential responses to such an unfamiliar and, for an untutored audience, outlandishly elaborate style.

Rehistoricizing the tradition: advocacy for the new through the old

This condition of in-betweenness is, from the perspective from which this chapter is written today, one of the most compelling contemporary aspects of Hsiung's migrant experience. His journey of self-translation did not end in complete – in the sense of unequivocally or uncritically performed – assimilation to the host culture but rather moved inexorably backwards and forwards between what he came to increasingly identify as his ancestor culture and his host world. The jobbing translator, whose original goal was to write a doctorate on Shakespeare and to continue the task of Chinese modernization by importing contemporary British writing in translation, now begins to wrestle with past and present, traditionalism and modernism, not as absolute categories but as inextricably and sinuously interwoven simultaneities. Hsiung left a country that he thought of as an anachronism in the modern world, both aloof and disregarded, but his experience of reification within the contours of a perceived radical alterity brought him as a translator in translation to the pain of the exclusions rooted in sustained misrecognition.

Here is one telling example of such misrecognition. At the start of *Lady Precious Stream*'s extraordinary run, it was rumoured that the author was Japanese, so that critics, based on this rumour, 'were naturally furious and thought they had been cheated' (Hsiung, 1973, p. 169). The bias here is rooted undoubtedly in the perception of the geopolitics of the Pacific Rim, where Japan was once again flexing its military might in the face of a China that seemed determined to shelter in its feudal past. Hsiung recalled that when he was introduced as the author of *Lady Precious Stream* to British writer and journalist John Otway Percy Bland (1863–1945), who had lived in China for 30 years, Bland declared the play must be Japanese, not believing that it could possibly have a Chinese author. Hsiung recorded his conversation with Bland as follows:

> This elderly English gentleman was mildly surprised to find the Chinese author did exist. [...] He asked: 'Can you speak Chinese?' I, like a fool or an innocent prisoner in the dock, tried my best to convince my questioner by answering in the affirmative and started to speak to him first in Mandarin and then in Southern dialect, without suspecting in the least that the man was doing his best to insult me. (Hsiung, 1973, p. 171)

What the incident disclosed to Hsiung was that he remained the characteristically untrustworthy other, a charge rooted not only in misrecognition but in the apparently wholesale dismissal of an entire country genetically incapable of producing anything of cultural value. The impostor's sense of guilt, of being caught like a criminal in the dock, is a typical symptom of his ingrained sense of not belonging, while the translator is wracked by anxiety that his work is swamped under the obduracy of misrecognition.

Hsiung was in this way forced to confront both personal and cultural exclusions that had profound geopolitical implications. The questions arise inevitably, therefore, as to which China he should translate to the West and what sort of translation might most effectively advocate for recognition. Lin Yutang (1895–1976), another key Chinese diasporic writer living in the United States at the same time as Hsiung lived in Britain, expresses this conflict beautifully as a developing crisis of perception:

> For the mass of foreground details, which swamps the foreign observer, swamps the modern Chinese as well. Perhaps he has even less the cool detachment of the foreign observer. In his breast is concealed a formidable struggle, or several struggles. There is the conflict between his ideal and his real China, and a more formidable conflict between his primaeval clan-pride and his moments of admiration for the stranger. His soul is torn by a conflict of loyalties belonging to opposite poles,

> a loyalty to old China, half romantic and half selfish, and a loyalty to open-eyed wisdom which craves for change and a ruthless clean-sweeping of all that is stale and putrid and dried up and mouldy. (Lin, 1936, p. 12)

In Hsiung's case, the contemporary China he intended to advocate for through his translation was in a hopeful state of transition between the feudalism of the past and the struggle for modernity in the present. So that, by the 1930s, even though the Republic of China had been founded nearly two decades earlier, and the feudal political system had been abolished 20 years previously with the aim of establishing a nation-wide system based on the democratic republicanism of the modern world, many cultural practices established over the centuries still coexisted in marked tension with these political, social and cultural aspirations. It was in this disputed territory between ongoing, unswerving tradition and modernizing tendencies that the New Culture Movement was born. As a student in the then Peking, Hsiung's intellectual life was galvanized by the Movement's radical critique of the classical Chinese traditions – including *xiqu* – as bulwarks of outdated convention, or being 'fogeyish', as Hu Shi (1891–1962), one of the leading figures of the New Cultural Movement, wrote disarmingly at the time (Hu, 2016, p. 178). As a burgeoning translator, therefore, Hsiung was totally persuaded by the argument that introducing and transplanting Western discourses of modernity, such as those of democracy and science, would create a 'new civilization' (Chen, 1919). But now, in London, Hsiung could no longer deny the weight of tradition in his own identity, both constructed and perceived. In some ways, he had always been aware of the tensions between ongoing traditions as a vital flow of cultural identity (not least arising from his love of *xiqu*) and the history-making projects of the New Culturists. That Hsiung saw tradition and history as dyadic is exemplified in his translation of *The Autobiography of Benjamin Franklin* (1929), which he elected to write in Classical Chinese, the complex form that New Culturalists argued needed to be replaced by the simpler vernacular form (白话文, see Hu, 1917).[2] Once in London, however, Hsiung's earlier attempts to defend the classical as a quiet act of resistance to the schematizing efforts of those who espoused a deracinating modernity now coalesced around an explicitly translational position in the life of one who had to face the heft of the Chinese classical tradition at the heart of his being, as a force within the ontology of the migrant. As he translated himself through his representation of the complexity of his cultural origins in the face of the essentializing tropes of Western colonial attitudes, Hsiung's work in translation becomes a profound meditation on the interplay between tradition and history, not solely in the thorny development of his country but at play in every cultural moment regardless of location.

At the heart of this dyad of tradition and history, there is a very different experience of time – time as the accumulated simultaneity of tradition, the embodiment of a synchronicity that offers its own conditions of psychological belonging (see, in this respect, Jung, 1960), and time as linear projection into the future, historical time that leads up to and away from a notional rupture between past and future, time as embodiment of the inexorable. As he considered his translation projects, Hsiung inevitably folded this nourishing sense of tradition as a flow of belonging into his aspiration for the modern, in a way that inevitably recalls how Michel de Certeau – again many years later, in his *The Writing of History* (1988) – was to distinguish between historiography as a source of power and tradition as an amalgam of forms and practices that embody the dominant experiences of social presence and individual, the animating forces of the social body itself (De Certeau, 1988, throughout).

Torn between the challenges of the present moment and his growing sense of absence from the wider assumptions of the Chinese 'social body', the migrant impostor teases out in his everyday experience ways that allow for some quality of the

---

[2] The new Simplified Chinese uses a register that is closer to spoken Chinese and is therefore much easier to read and understand, in contrast to what was regarded as the elitist use of Classical Chinese writing conventions.

connection between the forms and values of his ancestor culture and the workings of the new context. And, in turn, the translated translator finds ways of advocating for not only the validity of that tradition but its condition of aliveness. The theatre, with its immediacy of reception and the conditions of imaginative encounter that it promotes, was the perfect testing ground for a theatre method that was modernist in its concern with the demands of the present moment, but that also refused to abandon the living flow of tradition. Hsiung's early translations, *Lady Precious Stream* (1934), *Mencius Was a Bad Boy* (1934) and *The Romance of the Western Chamber* (1935), derive from Classical Chinese stories with roots in Confucianism. Among them, *Lady Precious Stream*, as we have already noted, and *The Romance of the Western Chamber* are the two acclaimed pieces drawn from the standard *xiqu* repertoire. Both feature archetypal storylines depicting the romance between a poor but gifted man and a noble-bred lady – reflecting classical Confucian teaching about pathways to success. *Mencius Was a Bad Boy* was a children's play adapted for the stage from a story familiar to children in China. 'The Mother of Mencius Moved Three Times' (孟母三迁) was originally included in the *Three Character Classic* (三字经), conceived of as Confucianist teachings for children composed in China around the twelfth century. In these translations/adaptations of classical works, Hsiung effectively emancipates translation from notions of source text primacy to become a mode of writing that advocates for recognition both of himself and for a China that is making history without abandoning the vivacity of its living traditions. It is a translation practice that acknowledges the presentism of the modernist writers so admired by Hsiung (he asked T. S. Eliot to write a short preface to *The Romance of the Western Chamber*), but at the same time does not shy away from a representation of the Chinese other in its own terms (which, at least partially perhaps, explains why Eliot refused Hsiung's request). The translated translator is, perhaps almost inevitably, staging his own experience of what Homi K. Bhabha (1994) was later to identify as hybridity: both the translator and the culture he is representing to his new audiences are blends of selfhood and of a nation that are simultaneously present and past.

In a reception context where his audience would inevitably interpret classical Chinese traditions, stories, ideas and art forms through the master discourse of an exoticized chinoiserie, Hsiung looks for ways of making these differences actually work on stage for his new audience through a rehistoricization, a reimagination of the relationship between the past and the present. The clear indebtedness to a modernist sense of the imperative of the present moment in *Lady Precious Stream* provides a portal through which the translator invites his audience into an unexpected encounter with the radical alterity of the Chinese tradition. One of the most prominent resulting changes, in this sense, is his redesign of the plot structure of the play. The original eight-excerpt performance is funnelled into a two-and-a-half-hour play based on four acts of two scenes each, more in keeping with the normal structure of West End plays at the time. In order to walk the audience through the storyline, he inserts 'lengthy descriptions of situation or character', which, tellingly, he declares in a newspaper interview that he has 'taken special pains to write informatively and yet with entertaining passages' (Hsiung, 1936). Hsiung's apparently throwaway concern with being 'entertaining' belies a carefully constructed strategy that reflects, for example, Pound's well-known (but so-called) translation of Chinese poems in *Cathay*, published in 1915. In *Cathay*, we still hear the echoes of Classical Chinese poems of the tenth century within the highly imagistic language that Pound adopts, but we can also clearly sense that these poems are written in a language thoroughly infused with Pound's inimitable style, language that is wholly refracted, wholly adapted, in a way that connects with current poetry traditions of contemporary English. In similar fashion, in terms of reworking the Chinese opera for his new audience in London, Hsiung adopts, although less wholeheartedly, a similar strategy that draws upon the modernist imperative of presentism, expressed in Pound's well-known exhortation of 1935 to 'make it new'. Similarly, Eliot, at the same time as Hsiung was translating, wrote his influential essay 'Tradition and the individual talent', one of whose central arguments is that 'novelty is better than repetition' (1982, p. 37). While Eliot, however, reconceptualizes tradition from the perspective of the present – see, for example, the first lines of his 'Burnt Norton', the opening section of *Four Quartets* – Hsiung's translation process was infused with a growing nostalgia towards a home that had already been left behind, with its living familiar traditions, and to reabsorbing these into the present moment. In this way, Hsiung mediates between his source texts' highly culture-specific and formulaic performance style, so temporally and spatially remote from his current target audience, and a theatre environment whose expectations had been honed by the forms of its dominant repertoire and generally colonial assumptions of culturally self-contained spectatorship.

In choosing to negotiate these classical Chinese stories with a London audience, Hsiung did not see any contradiction with his simultaneous desire to present China as an emerging modern nation with long cultural roots. The competing demands of the informative and the entertaining, which he referred to in his interview, are popularizing abbreviated accounts for a translation procedure that, in terms of the stage practice that it enshrines, refuses to grant authority to either context of reception or originating source. In the same spirit of translational mobility, he presents his interpretation of ancient China as much more than a showcase of traditional Chinese aesthetics, but also as a new platform for 1930s China, which, importantly, his experience had led him to recognize as one of the West's global series of misrecognized others. On the one hand, he recognized that translations are written for new audiences, a practical approach to theatre-making that is sustained by both political and modernist arguments for breaking with the past, so that *Lady Precious Stream* is designed to be present to the new audience – in Hsiang's key term, entertainingly grafted onto their experience and assumptions. But, on the other hand, the classical Chinese tradition that these plays derive from works on stage as living heritage, both counterbalancing the translator's sense of absence of a psychological home and advocating for the understanding of homeplace in a new context. Put simply, the act of translation in this way provides a working model of encounter, which is both deeply personal, in that Hsiung's translation of *Lady Precious Stream* is not a relinquishing of the living flow of Chinese tradition but a form of nostalgia for his ancestor traditions in a new country and politically and culturally astute in the complex stage negotiations between source and target contexts that it carefully engineers. In that way, *Lady Precious Stream*, as the most representative and indeed most successful in audience terms of his translations, emerges from a hybridized translation method that rests upon a confluence of the flow of the classical Chinese tradition with modernist presentism. While the form of the translation conforms to London audience expectations, Hsiung subverts and defamiliarizes it with the incorporation of specific and carefully negotiated elements drawn from the Chinese tradition, so that his audience can enter the unfamiliar world of China through channels with which they are already familiar. It is this interplay between the familiar and the unfamiliar that Hsiung, assiduously attending every possible production in London, knew to be the main cognitive method of theatre.

Resistant translation: advocacy against othering

Emily Apter (2007) proposes resistant translation as a way of maintaining the heterogeneity of local cultures struggling to assert their uniqueness in the face of the homogenizing trends of globalization and enforced hegemony. At the heart of the discussion of the politics of recognition (see, for example, Taylor, 1994) there is a clear concern with the translational power of acts of representation, a concern that Hsiung had already intuited. In this way, his work also anticipates the hugely influential movement of the cultural interweaving of performance cultures that is spearheaded by Erika Fischer-Lichte (see, for example, her 2014 edited collection of essays *The Politics of Interweaving Performance Cultures: Beyond postcolonialism*), whose key method, developed to mitigate cultural appropriation, broadly proposes splicing the performance and production assumptions of the source into those of the target context – see Xu and Johnston (2022) and Johnston and Xu (2021) for a discussion of the possible interweaving of *xiqu* with the Spanish Golden Age *comedia*.

In the 1930s, both China and Chinese plays were constructed or consumed within the tastes of exoticism – which this essay has characterized as a function of chinoiserie – relegating the country and its representatives (as the migrant Hsiung realized he inevitably was) to a peripheral position as a dimly glimpsed but widely misrecognized other in 1930s London. After he finished the translation of *Lady Precious Stream*, Hsiung tried to find a competent producer, but discovered that the biggest barrier for him at that time and in that place was his Chinese identity:

> **Experience told me that my personal appearance had much to do with all these rejections because very few people believed – and there are many who still doubt – that this play was authentic Chinese when they had had the unfortunate experience of meeting the author.** (Hsiung, 1973, p. 164)

The emphasis on appearance is interesting. Clearly, Hsiung's young Chinese face was perceived less as a stimulus for theatre managers to believe in the play's unusual commitment to truthfulness and more as a racial barrier to acceptance within the London theatre business world. As a commercial enterprise, this then perpetrated the crass commodification of China in a series of so-called 'yellow face' plays from the pens of exoticizing English-speaking writers, such as the hugely successful *The Yellow Jacket* (1916) and *The Circle of Chalk* (1924), plays that Bernard Shaw referred to disparagingly as 'Chinatown plays' (Shaw in Tian, 2017, p. 158) in which China was ridiculed as a land of exotic figures, curious beliefs and barbaric social practices. Hsiung was, of course, determined to secure the fame and success that would promote his social acceptance, but the painful rejection prompted by his racial identity and the marginalized position of China on the London stage reminded him that his translation also had to serve as a medium of resistance to the Anglosphere's routine exoticization of the Chinese-speaking world. Translation, for Hsiung, becomes a cultural practice that by promoting the conditions of the encounter between both worlds might serve as a source of more equitable recognition.

Translation is at its very best when it refuses to assign moral, political, cultural and discursive superiority to source and target contexts alike and can advocate powerfully for such recognition. In this, and in other ways, this chapter has attempted to suggest that Hsiung was ahead of his time as a translator and that his thinking was ignited by his perception of the stereotypical elements of racial discrimination he experienced as a Chinese person in England. As he noted painfully, one of these enduring stereotypes portrays the Chinese as 'sinister monster' (Hsiung, 1973, p. 185), frequently leading to the casting of Chinese as the villains in 'horror and mystery plays', such as 'Fu Manchu, and Amah in *East of Suez*' (Hsiung, 1973, p. 185). Such characterization is accompanied by features that function as external manifestations of utter and incommunicable alterity, inhuman, animal-like features like 'a pair of smallish eyes which, when open, are only semi-open' and with 'extremely high cheek bones, protruding teeth almost like tusks, and his head is generally deeply sunken between his shoulders' and 'a long queue [presumably pigtails or a ponytail] and very long fingernails resembling claws of birds of prey' (Hsiung, 1973, p. 185). Hsiung, once again, resorts to a characteristically detoxicating sense of humour, but Richard Kearney is more pointedly political in his view that the reason people construct alien representations of the other arises from what is in the first instance a rooted fear of radical difference and what all too easily is transformed by the imagination through processes of uglification and simplification soon to harden into sources of hostility (Kearney, 2002, p. 5). Dehumanizing the other frequently operates through channels of aggression, sublimated and actual.

Always mindful of Mei Langfang's description of his American tour as a work of cultural ambassadorship, Hsiung thought of translation in this way as work of consummate cultural utility. One of the most notable ways in which he seeks to secure this objective of mutual understanding is to create a new character in the acting edition of *Lady Precious Stream* – the Honourable Reader, who is responsible for briefly explaining stage conventions and narrative outlines to the audience before each act. In Brechtian stagings, such a character would function as a narrator, but Hsiung has no interest in alienating his audience or distancing them from the Chinese sources of action on stage in front of them.[3] His goal is based entirely on the force of complicity, so that in terms of storytelling, the Honourable Reader fills in the gaps in the audience's knowledge about the complex codes and conventions of Peking Opera performance and walks them through the intricacy of plots and narrative structure. In this way, put simply, the translator ensures that misunderstanding does not preclude spectator complicity, creating through this new role the live embodiment of an onstage translator who advocates not only for Peking Opera but for nuanced representations of China itself. This new role stakes Hsiung's claim to be presenting nuanced representations of China, a claim of what today should be seen as his legitimacy to 'tell China's story' (as in Xi Jinping's speech of 19 August 2013). In the follow-up Broadway production of the play in 1936, in order to further mitigate cultural appropriation on the part of the audience, Hsiung cast Mei Mei Sze, the daughter of the current Chinese ambassador in New York, to perform this role. This particular Honorable (in the American spelling) Reader with a Chinese face and fluent English highlights the aspiration of recognition that the role embodies and that, in Hsiung's own words, helps him to 'put China on the map' (Hsiung in Zheng, 2015, p. 289). At the heart of this creation of a resistant translation is Hsiung's reconceptualization and the

[3] Interestingly, Mei's 1935 Soviet Union tour brought Peking Opera to the attention of European critics and practitioners of film and theatre. Among them, one of the most visionary theatre practitioners was Bertolt Brecht, who wrote about the non-naturalistic acting-centred style of Peking Opera in terms of an embodiment of 'alienation' techniques. Notably, he identified this special technique in terms immediately reminiscent of his own emerging theory of *Verfremdung*, praising Peking Opera's eschewing of realism as 'an artful and artistic act of self-estrangement' (Brecht, 1961, p. 131).

way he dramatizes the key relationship between self and other. Hsiung, as we have seen, refused to see this as a simple binary and instead complicates the relationship between the occidental located self and the oriental dislocated other, beyond the conventional orientalist representations that London audiences were much more familiar with. The interpretation and subsequent representation of otherness is a central concern of translators, especially where the aspiration of the translation in question is to engineer some measure of conversation between the cultures in question. The interpretation of otherness in Hsiung's translation is widened, in this case, to become a crucial territory where he incorporates the reception world into this deeply emotive encounter between self and other. This interplay of self and other is key to his resistant translation. It was a world, after all, in which, as we have seen, he himself was treated in terms of radical alterity.

The original story of *Lady Precious Stream* deals with the wars between central China and Xi Liang (西涼), a kingdom on the north-western Chinese periphery, more or less in Central Asia today. At the time of the play's action, Xi Liang was considered the embodiment of otherness, so that in Hsiung's translation what now becomes the Western Region is notionally located somewhere in Europe. The people of this Western Region are now described through the stereotypes of Europeans found in classical Chinese literature, allowing the Honourable Reader at the beginning of Act Three to inform the audience: 'All, male and female, have red hair, green eyes, prominent noses, and hairy hands' (Hsiung, 1949, p. 78). It is a carnivalesque device designed to turn the tables on the audience, to make them feel that the character is now holding a distorting mirror up to them (see, in this regard, Bakhtin, 1984, pp. 71–2). Hsiung's description of the Western Region's inhabitants is no less rooted in Chinese classical literature, drawing upon ancient sources rather than the freedom of his own creative imagination. In that way, his translation of China to London draws on a series of intertextual references – his description of the inhabitants of the Western Regions as people with 'red hair', for example, dates back to the imaginings in classical Chinese literature of Europeans as the 'red-hair fan' (红毛番), where the fan refers to a fierce animal with sharp claws. The term itself originally was applied to Dutch invaders on the south coast of China in the fifteenth century, so called because they 'dress in red, with red hair all over their body, with feet and toes twice as big as ours, and much stronger than us' (Guo, 1599, my translation). The subversion here, by which China is positioned as the located self and the West is now regarded as the dislocated misrepresented other, cleverly reverses the context of reception. In this case, rather than operating through the simple binary of self and other, what the audience sees on stage and experiences in terms of encounter is a subverted relationship which not only ushers them into an experience of the excitement of difference within the liminal space of the theatre event but also, importantly, discloses the translator's intention to enter into some sort of humorous dialogue that marks a strategy of resistance to exoticization and othering. Such exaggerated emphases on the strangeness of the appearance of the people from the West echoes, of course, similar clichéd conceptions in the West about the 'barbarians of the North', and while London audiences would in all likelihood have remained oblivious to the roots of Hsiung's referencing, he still manages to communicate something of what the returned gaze might see.

Conclusion

This chapter has attempted to uncover the roots of a translation method whose motor force is that of advocacy. Before coming to England, in the context of the culture wars of 1930s China Hsiung had developed a clear and, it must be said, uncomplicated sense of the ways in which translated texts can help to profile a society and, by importing alternative constructions from the world outside, may contribute to healthy debate. In the wake of his sense of dislocation in England, he honed and extended this sense of utility, of what we might think of as the big work of translation, so that in his eyes it becomes a cultural practice that can advocate for recognition and understanding. Hsiung's overall strategy and subsequent choices support his objective of creating plays that simultaneously spoke of the riches of the Chinese cultural past while at the same time addressing identifiable sources of potential misrecognition for his English-speaking audiences. Hsiung's new method of translating China to his London spectators is crucial to representing fairly both his own culture and himself – as one who has been pressganged by circumstances into being regarded as a metonymy of that culture. This is what he means by putting China on the map as an equitable cultural other to the anglophone world. Translation, in this case, serves as a possible bridging zone between China and the West, a possibility that the translated translator yearns for from their in-between position. This is translation at its most culturally and, indeed, politically persuasive, where the translator is visibly embodied as an advocate for a new China on stage. Such advocacy through translation is extraordinary because, as a Chinese national, Hsiung also asserted himself as an English-language writer and, in later life, determined international activist, for whom translation was a key mode for the promotion of understanding in a context beset by cultural stereotypes and political misrecognition.

References

Apter, E. (2007) Untranslatable? The 'reading' versus the 'looking'. *Journal of Visual Culture*, 6 (1), 149–56.

Bakhtin, M. (1984) *Rabelais and His World*. Bloomington, IN: Indiana University Press.

Bhabha, H. K. (1994) *The Location of Culture*. London: Routledge.

Brecht, B. (1961) On Chinese acting. Trans. E. Bentley, *The Tulane Drama Review*, 6 (1), 130–6.

Certeau, M. de (1988) *The Writing of History*. Trans. Tom Conlet. New York: Columbia University Press.

Chen, D. (1919) 本志罪案签辩书 (A defence to the original crimes). *New Youth*, 1 (6). Available from: https://www.marxists.org/

chinese/chenduxiu/marxist.org-chinese-chen-19190115.htm (Accessed: 1 March 2023).

Eliot, T. S. (1982) Tradition and the individual talent. *Perspecta*, 19, 36–42.

Fischer-Lichte, E. (2014) Introduction, in Fischer-Lichte, E., Jost, T. and Iris Jain, S. (eds), *The Politics of Interweaving Performance Cultures: Beyond postcolonialism*. New York and London: Routledge.

Goldstein, J. (2007) *Drama Kings: Players and publics in the re-creation of Peking Opera*. Berkeley, CA, Los Angeles, CA, and London: University of California Press.

Guo, P. (1599) 广东通志 (Guang Dong Annuals). Available from: https://ctext.org/wiki.pl?if=gb&res=341768&remap=gb (Accessed: 1 March 2023).

Hawley, K. (2019) What is impostor syndrome? *Aristotelian Society Supplementary Volume*, 93 (1), 203–26. DOI: https://doi.org/10.1093/arisup/akz003.

Hsiung, S. (1929) 富兰克林自传 (*The Autobiography of Benjamin Franklin*). Beijing: Commercial Press.

— (1930) 可敬的克莱登 (*The Admirable Crichton*). Shanghai: Commercial Press.

— (1931) 彼得潘 (*Peter Pan*). The Short Story Magazine.

— (1934) Some conventions of the Chinese stage. *People's National Theatre Magazine*, 3–5.

— (1935) Mammon. *The People's Tribune (Shanghai)*, 8 (2), 125–51.

— (1936) Occidental fantasy: Dr. Hsiung cites the West's reacting to 'Lady Precious Stream', *The New York Times*, 9 February.

— (1946) Through Eastern eyes, in Winsten, S. (ed), *G.B.S. 90: Aspects of Bernard Shaw's Life and Work*. London: Hutchinson, pp. 194–9.

— (ed) (1949) Introduction, *Lady Precious Stream: An Old Chinese play done into English according to its traditional style* (8th edn). London: Methuen, pp. xv–xvii.

— (1968) *The Romance of the Western Chamber*. New York and London: Columbia University Press.

— (ed) (1973) Afterthought, *The Professor from Peking*. Taibei: Zhongyang Books Press, pp. 163–98.

— (2010) 八十回忆 (The memoirs in my 80s). Beijing: Dolphin Books.

Hu, S. (1917) 文学改良刍议 (An initial discussion on the reformation of literature). Available from: https://zh.wikipedia.org/zh-hans/文学改良刍议

— (2016) 文学进化观念与戏剧改良 (The concept of literature evolution and theatre improvement), in Zhao, B. (ed), 新青年: 文学批评卷 (*New Youth Magazine: The Volume of Literature Criticism*), 5, 176–88. Beijing, Zhengzhou: Hena Literature and Art Press. https://zh.wikisource.org/wiki/文学进化观念与戏剧改良

Johnston, D. and Xu, L. (2021) Ecologies of translation: Chinese classical opera and Spanish Golden Age theatre. *Boletín de la Biblioteca de Menéndez Pelayo*, 97, 197–224.

Jung, C. G. (1960) *Synchronicity: An acausal connecting principle* (Volume 8, *The Collected Works of CG Jung*). Princeton, NJ: Princeton University Press.

Kearney, R. (2002) *Strangers, Gods and Monsters: Interpreting otherness*. London and New York: Routledge.

Lin, Y. (1936) *My Country and My People*. London: William Heinemann.

Pound, E. (1915) *Cathay*. London: Elkin Mathews.

— (1935) *Make It New: Essays by Ezra Pound*. New Haven, CT: Yale University Press.

Qi, R. (2015) 论戏剧来源于古之歌舞 (On theatre originates from ancient singing and dancing). In Qi, R. 齐如山国剧论从 (Qi Rushan's comments on national play in series). Beijing: Commercial Press, pp. 55–61.

Qi, R. 齐如山国剧论从 (Qi Rushan's comments on national play in series). Beijing: Commercial Press.

Qi, R. (2015) 齐如山谈梅兰芳 (Qi Rushan talks about Mei Lanfang). Beijing: Culture and Art Publishing House.

Rushdie, S. (1992) *Imaginary Homelands: Essays and criticism 1981–1991*. New York: Penguin Books.

Taylor, C. (1994) The politics of recognition, in Gutmann, A. (ed), *Multiculturalism: Examining the politics of recognition*. Princeton, NJ: Princeton University Press, pp. 25–73.

Taylor, G. (1991) *Reinventing Shakespeare: A cultural history from the Restoration to the present*. Oxford and New York: Oxford University Press.

Tian, M. (2017) Lady Precious Stream: A Chinese chinoiserie anglicized on the modern British stage. *Comparative Drama*, 51 (2), 158–86.

Xi, J. (2013) 全国宣传思想工作会议讲话 (Speech at the national publicity and ideology meeting). *XinhuaNet*. Available from: https://www.xinhuanet.com/zgjx/2013-08/21/c_132648439.htm (Accessed: 3 November 2023).

Xu, L. and Johnston, D. (2022) Between safeguarding and translating: Chinese classical opera and Spanish Golden Age theatre. *Translation Studies*, 15 (3), 323–39. DOI: 10.1080/14781700.2022.2120906.

Zheng, D. (2015) Performing transposition: Lady Precious Stream on Broadway. *New England Theatre Journal*, 26, 83–102. Available from: https://search.proquest.com/docview/1789380729/abstract/3BF6B5BE5F7F43 EEPQ/1 (Accessed: 1 March 2023).

6

Advocating intercultural dialogue through translating artist-activist practice

Sophie Stevens

Overview

The chapter identifies the ways in which translation challenges us to expand and modify our perspectives on the world. As a translator and researcher, I see my role as analysing, interrogating and unlocking the multiplicity of experiences, voices, ideas, imagined worlds and discourses present in the source text and then enlivening them in the target language so that the target audience can also experience this multiplicity. When analysing and translating artist-activist ideas, performances and slogans in the context of workshops with students, the challenge and invitation to view the world differently and confront new ways of thinking is paramount. This is because both activism and translation can decentre students' experience by challenging them to put themselves in the position of the other. By exploring translation as a process of research, a mode of cultural production and a way of understanding intercultural dialogue, this chapter advocates for translation practice as a way to cultivate cultural inquiry into artist-activist practices. It proposes that as teacher-translator-academic, we can navigate the challenges posed by dealing with these topics by advocating for translation as a mode of critical understanding.

> **The admission of approximation is necessary, for one cannot hope to be absolute in his precision. He cannot see, or even conceive of a thing from all possible points of view, simultaneously.**
>
> Alexander Calder, A propos of measuring a mobile, unpublished manuscript, 7 October 1943. Calder Foundation archives at *Calder-Picasso* exhibition (2019).

Introduction: translation and multiplicity

Translation is a complex activity for many reasons, but perhaps the most significant is that it asks us to attempt to see a text, and the world that text creates or refers to, from a range of perspectives at the same time. In the first instance, translation asks us to encounter the text from the points of view of reader and audience and as we experience the text, to engage with the images and worlds it creates. We imagine where the text has originated and where the target language might take it and this sparks questions which are explored through a process of research. Ultimately, translation asks us to place ourselves in the position of author, or as Lydia Davis suggests, 'ventriloquist and chameleon' (2021, p. 15), as we render it in the target language. Multiplicity is at the heart of the translation process precisely because it asks us to view the text, the world and ourselves as multiple – as new perspectives are opened up through the text. This chapter examines the significance of this multiplicity and the possibilities that it offers when translating artist-activist texts, performances and slogans in workshops with students. Both activism and translation can decentre students' experience by challenging them to adopt a new, unfamiliar perspective. This chapter proposes that as teacher-translator-academic, we can navigate and support students in gaining an understanding of activist topics through advocating for translation as a mode of critical inquiry. I seek to explore how translation as a process of research provides a methodology for analysing, understanding and translating the specificities of activism. By enabling students to engage with the translation process, we can use the language of a source text as a route into exploring the multiple meanings that it generates in the source and target cultures. While we cannot constantly view a text, play or performance simultaneously from different perspectives, this chapter argues that a workshop setting offers a space for encountering the text and revealing and exploring multiple ideas about it. I show how we can use the questions generated through interrogating the language of the source text as the basis for research questions which enable us to broaden our understanding of the source culture and the connections that can be established with the target culture. I explore ways in which different aspects of the translation process open up a dialogue between cultures which is complex and enriching, and can allow for new modes of understanding both ourselves and others.

Translation shapes new perspectives

I primarily work on theatre and performance texts which were originally written in Spanish, and I translate into English. When I translate, I analyse, interrogate and seek to unlock the multiplicity of experiences, voices, ideas, imagined worlds and discourses present in the source text, to then enliven them in the target language so that the target audience can also experience this multiplicity. Texts rarely say just one thing and by analysing in depth the range of voices present in the source text, I gain an understanding of the network of meanings, ideas and conflicts generated by the original. I start to make connections with the target context, usually a British one, and the discourses and conversations taking place in that context. I start to ask the following questions about the text: how might it resonate in Britain today, and specifically in London where I am based? What are the links between source and target culture? How can a dialogue begin on stage and then extend into the audience, sparking new conversations, in the target context? At every stage in the process, questions are generated, so that I undertake a process of 'bombard[ing] it with questions from the target language's point of view' (Pavis, 1992, p. 138) in a way which seeks not to find all the answers but to explore the multiple possible ones and explore the new questions that these questions generate in the target context so that a connection is formed with the target audience. From my position in the target context, analysing the source dramatic text, I view this as a process of extension, of extending my arms out into the world, through this text, and reaching out and making links. The text can enable me to connect with those who might have shared, for example, a similar experience of exclusion, undergone the same kind of political upheaval, feared a repressive leader, or struggled in a similar way with the choices made by previous generations. By reaching out, seeking and seeing ideas and experiences that I can establish connections with, I also, inevitably, encounter difference. Therefore, a key feature of this process of extension is that it is also necessarily a process of experiencing newness. As I reach out and find connections, at the same time I also encounter new perspectives and ways of looking at and imagining the world. I find ways of reasoning that I had not come across before because they are linked to the specific place from which they emerged, and I also find ideas, words and actions that challenge me, shock me and expose me to attitudes that surprise me and ignite new ideas.

One of the ways in which I conceptualize this process and experience of cultural encounter through texts is as if reaching out my arms and encountering, feeling, a shape that seems familiar. However, then, as I begin to explore it more, I come to realize that it has a different side that I had never seen before and perhaps never even considered a possibility. This new side is connected to the other sides, and it fits perfectly, if somewhat surprisingly to me, just where it is. And by encountering it in this way, I am challenged to think about how it is integrated into the shape, how it contributes to it but, from where I am, also expands it. This new side acts in the same way that cultural encounters through translation do as they offer and ask us to consider new perspectives on topics or situations that we might already feel familiar with. The shape has been expanded and I have encountered something new. This shape allows me to experience something sort-of familiar and at the same time this is something new, which exists as a complex multi-sided entity. One of the reasons that I chose to start this chapter with a description of a mobile is because the idea that it gives us of shape is useful, as is the idea that it conjures up in our imagination of movement, change and transformation. As the mobile moves, we become aware of different aspects of its make-up. The quotation reminds us that the construction of the mobile, like translation, demands and complicates the need for multiple perspectives.

An essential awareness that we should strive to engage with and create in the target language the multiple perspectives, qualities and ideas of the source text underpins the translator's work. As does an awareness that we cannot achieve all these objectives at all times, and so the translator must make choices at every stage in the process, based on their research, understanding and interaction with the text. At times, this might feel like just an approximation, but it is one that has been informed by a process of questioning, research and investigation. This chapter proposes that the context of the translation workshop is particularly effective in facilitating this explorative stage in the translation process. The workshop creates a space for multiple perspectives and the generation of research questions. In the workshop we enact a methodology of translation as research to enables us to negotiate activist material. As teacher-translator-academic, we can advocate for translation as a way to create an intercultural encounter through engaging with artist-activist work. This chapter uses the case study of introducing activist performance into a workshop setting to propose strategies for advocating for translation as a mode for critical inquiry and to show how this type of advocacy can create new perspectives on activist practice originating in other cultures and languages.

Translating activist hashtags and performance

In this section, I show how introducing the artivist (activism through art) performance intervention, *La caída de las campanas* (The falling of the bells), created by Uruguayan artist, activist and scholar Hekatherina Delgado into a workshop setting provides a case study for employing translation as a process of research and critical inquiry. *La caída de las campanas* was a performance created in 2015 and enacted regularly in the streets of Montevideo, in public places, in response to feminicides occurring in Uruguay. Between 2015 and 2017, Delgado and a group of collaborators took to the streets and performed the intervention every time a woman was murdered as a result of gender-based violence. The performances were often recorded through photographs and videos and uploaded to social media sites, primarily Facebook, so the performance could be rewatched. Recordings were often accompanied by hashtags and slogans associated with the feminist movement in Uruguay, Latin America and beyond. I frequently encountered the slogan *#TocanAUnaTocanATodas* and I have brought it into workshop settings with students, and in the following section I will demonstrate how translating this hashtag can equip students to critically analyse the performance.

The fact that the performance was recorded means that I can share clips from it in workshops and classes, and on occasions students have recognized the significance of the issue of gender-based violence but felt unsure about how to discuss the issue or the ways in which *La caída de las campanas* functions to draw attention to, critique and rethink this issue. Therefore, I have used the following as a starting question: how can translating *#TocanAUnaTocanATodas*, which so often accompanies the recordings, help us to think critically about the performance? A first translation might be: touch one of us, touch all of us. This is because *tocar* means to touch. In thinking about it in the context of gender-based violence, we can go further to specify how *tocar* can also suggest violence or abuse and so the resonances can be expanded when we understand how it engages with the concerns of the performance. This can also be a productive starting point for creating new ways of analysing the performance itself. This is because, while these associations to physical violence are evoked, the performers in the piece move their bodies in a way which does not represent violence but demonstrates a clear connection to each other, to the urban performance setting and to the instruments that they use.

Tocar can also mean to play an instrument. A key feature of *La caída de las campanas* is the use of hand bells to create noise and rhythm and draw attention to the performers. This provokes the question as to how this hashtag, used alongside the performance, is another mechanism to draw attention to the significance of the bells that the performers use. It can provide a route into analysing the ways in which the performers play or play with the bells. Focusing on this meaning of *tocar* shifts our attention, perspective and ways of analysing the piece away from the perpetrators of violence – who were, in effect, the trigger for this artivist response – and onto the agency and activism of the performers. This generates further questions: Why choose bells? What do they add to the piece? How are they used? Do they symbolize something in the Uruguayan context? What do they symbolize beyond in other contexts? Through a close analysis of the language used alongside this performance, we can use translation as a mode of inquiry to critically analyse and comment upon both the piece itself and the possibilities for translation. Furthermore, by placing this hashtag in dialogue with the performance, I am already demonstrating to students one way that we understand and study the relationship between language and culture in translation. In the first instance, the performance becomes the context for this short hashtag text, so this constitutes a first step in researching the context of the original. The questions that arise then ask us to examine the broader context and to conduct research into the Uruguayan and Latin American contexts of activism, gender-based violence and performance.

Tocar has multiple meanings; this is not unusual for a word. Engaging with language by exploring and thinking through the multiple terms and meanings that this verb generates in a workshop context opens up new perspectives on the work. It also creates a productive and fruitful way to identify and work through research questions and their cultural implications. This is because the workshop offers a space in which multiplicity and dialogue can be fostered. In her study of the ways in which the disciplinary boundaries between creative writing and translation are porous, Cecilia Rossi draws on the work of Roger Sederat to specify that two key characteristics of the Literary Translation Workshop are 'ongoing dialogue' and 'collaborative process' (2018, p. 52). Rossi is referring to later stages in the process, when students might seek feedback on translations that they have produced, and this is significant because it reflects the openness, discursiveness and creativity which permeate the literary translation process to which the workshop contributes. The workshop focusing on translation as a route into interrogating activist practice and material encompasses these key qualities in order to create a space in which to generate and exchange ideas and perspectives to understand the complexity of an activist performance intervention.

What about *una* and *todas*? One and all. One woman; all women (because *una* is grammatically feminine). Analysing this part of the hashtag enables us to specify and articulate the significance of collective action and intervention as fundamental to the way in which the performance functions as activism through art. We can read this emphasis on the collective, present throughout the process of creating the performance, because Delgado invites performers to join her for each intervention, as juxtaposed with the use of *tocan* in the third-person plural of the verb. The use of 'they' at the start of the phrase and 'all women' at the end is striking. We can ask what kind of relationships it sets up; it seems to create contrast between them and us. And who might 'them' and 'us' denote, include and exclude? The hashtag has also been modified to *#TocanAUneTocanATodes*. The use of 'e' is one of the ways in which Spanish speakers have sought to disrupt gendered forms of language to create more inclusive forms. This is significant because it can be used as a starting point for a discussion on how activism can transform the ways in which language is used. We can also consider how the impact of this transformation can be amplified through translation as it has repercussions on how other languages are used. The attention to these details sparks questions as to why collective action is part of activist practice and we can begin to draw links to other activist interventions in Latin America. We can understand links, but we can also ask what the specificities of collective action are in the Uruguayan context. What is the relationship there between the 'one' and 'all'? *La caída de las campanas* specifically protested the murder of women – or feminicide – so the collective response shows how the loss of one woman affects others – multiple women. Loss is a concept presented in the hashtag used throughout Latin America since 2015, *#NiUnaMenos* (#NotOneWomanLess), which gained international recognition, meaning that some students might recognize it. This sparks research questions about the resonances and connections around these ideas of loss. If both of the hashtags are both about loss, then what are the similarities and differences?

One way to respond to this question is through further research by reading the work of Marcela A. Fuentes on hashtag activism. In considering the two slogans/hashtags alongside one another and the functions that they serve as short provocative texts, we can develop new insights into the messages that they communicate and which would need to be transferred into an English translation. In *Ni Una Menos* as hashtag and slogan, I had always focused on the significance of every woman and previously proposed a translation of 'Every Woman Counts'. However, Fuentes's discussion of loss sparks ideas about how this hashtag and slogan connects to the goals of *Ni Una Menos* as a movement: the slogan seeks to enact a future in which not a single woman is missing, and she uses the translation I used above: '#NotOneWomanLess' (2019, p. 174). It therefore functions not only as a response to loss but also as a demand for an imagined future where no more women are lost to gender-based violence. Once again, thinking through language in translation changes our perspective on the function and dynamism of these short texts, this time by asking us to consider how *Ni Una Menos* looks to the future. If *Ni Una Menos* can signal a future without violence, can other hashtags and performances also do this? The performance of *La caída de las campanas* is marked by its ephemerality, as are other theatre and performance events, and the hashtag *#TocanAUnaTocanATodas* is in the present tense, which can be seen to form a connection to the ways in which the pieces are re-enacted in response to the murder of each woman in the present day. Does the lack of verbs in *#NiUnaMenos* detach it from the temporal restrictions in a way that enables us to use it to imagine and open up possibilities for a future without violence? How might we capture this in an English translation? By considering these questions in a workshop, we begin to think creatively about the functions of hashtags and slogans. At the same time, we begin to critically examine the ways in which activism has a key role in questioning and critiquing the present and sparking ways for us to imagine the future. Translation as a mode of inquiry instigates these forms of analysis to enable us to examine artistic-activist practice, how activism links to action and new ways of conceptualizing these functions.

I have also applied the term 'feminicide' in my analysis so far. This is a translation of the Spanish term – *feminicidio* – introduced into academic discussions in 1987 through the work of Mexican scholar, activist, politician and lawyer María Marcela Lagarde y de los Ríos as a way to specify and theorize the factors that contribute to the killing of women because they are women. It therefore seeks to theoretically and linguistically expand the term 'femicide' used in English to refer to the murder of women. *Feminicidio* is used to refer to the killing of women both *because* they are women *and* because of the structures and inequalities within society that enable violence against women to exist, so it seeks to always and necessarily refer to systemic violence (Fregoso and Bejarano, 2010, p. 5). In her keynote at the 2021 Association of Hispanists of Great Britain and Ireland Annual Conference Online, Professor Nuala Finnegan discussed translating the lyrics that form part of the 2019 activist intervention *Un violador en tu camino* (A Rapist in Your Path) by Chilean feminist collective LasTesis into English and other languages. She specified some of the challenges that she and her collaborators faced in translating the term *feminicidio* which appears in the chant that is part of the performance. In her lecture, in searching to understand and articulate the difficulty not only of translating but also of saying aloud this term, Finnegan (2021) raised the question: what is the work that that extra syllable does when we use it in English, so when we speak of feminicide rather than femicide?

I argue that Finnegan (2021) ascribes a predominantly performative function to this term by suggesting that the extra syllable works in the following ways: to mark the excess of violence; to create an extra space which inverts a power balance and recognizes women's voices by pushing back against multiple forms of silencing; to create an afterlife for those women who have died as a result of violence. Both Finnegan in her lecture and I in this chapter are examining the role of this word in multiple activist contexts, including the context of activism through performance. Therefore, by identifying a performative function to the extra syllable in *feminicidio*/feminicide, and the way in which it functions to interrupt and disrupt, we can identify how it intersects with the ways in which activist performance interventions also function to disrupt narratives and the voices that dominate these narratives – to speak out on behalf of victims of gender-based violence, to commemorate and to create a space for collective responses (see Stevens, 2020, for a detailed study of the disruptive and commemorative function of *La caída de las campanas*). Examining and working to understand this term which emerges from the context, scholarship and activism of Latin America introduces students to ways of theorizing violence against women in Latin America. Focusing on the performative function, the potential for unlocking new ideas, and the possible challenges when translating *feminicidio* provides new insights and ways of critiquing activist performance. Bringing this term into the discussion about the performance *La caída de las campanas* and hashtag *#TocanAUnaTocanATodas*, and using translation as a mode of critical inquiry to explore it, enables students to broaden their understanding of the specificities of violence against women in the context of Latin America and to begin to think about the connections to the target context, in which they are located, thus sparking a dialogue across cultures. By using translation as part of a research methodology to unpick and unpack #*TocanAUnaTocanATodas* in dialogue with the performance, as well as critical terms, we explore and critically discuss how hashtags and performances are creative tools for simultaneously representing and embodying presence and loss.

The workshop setting: language, embodiment and space in between

When we are in the role of teachers and facilitators, we can advocate for translation as the starting point for a methodology for studying activist practice in seminars and workshops; in doing this, we enable and activate the process of translation as research. In this section, I understand the workshop using translation as a critical methodology as a space for collaboration, exchange and experimentation, and that all students and participants take part in these activities as part of the initial stages of analysing the material. By advocating for translation as a critical methodology, we create new ways for teachers, facilitators and students to engage with activist material. This allows teachers and facilitators to occupy a position from which we can negotiate some of the complexities of working with activist material which also intersect with some of the complexities of advocacy itself (and raised in the introduction to this volume): who are we advocating for? On behalf of? Because of? This is because one of the challenges of presenting activist material in any teaching or learning situation is that often it is understood that we become a spokesperson for a particular activist, activist practice or the concerns that they raise. As teacher and facilitator, we may start to feel as if we speak on their behalf or advocate for them. In some cases, we may want to.

To return to the idea of 'them and us' introduced in the case study hashtag in this chapter, we may take on a responsibility for establishing these categories in order to get the force of the activist practice across, and we might feel obliged to assert our own position, which, in turn, can make students feel obliged to do the same. This can shift the focus and disrupt the learning environment because it moves our attention away from the activist practice that we want to interrogate, explore and critique. Students do need to have a clear idea of what is at stake both within the performance piece and for the performers themselves within the society and context in which the activism takes place. In the case of the examples studied here, students need to develop an awareness of the prevalence of gender-based violence and the issues, ideologies and legislation with which this interacts in the Latin American source context. But while some introductory information can be provided by the teacher facilitator as a starting point, this can also be a topic for further research as a way to contextualize the piece. This shifts the position that we occupy as teachers and facilitators and also paves the way for students to conduct independent research. If we want to create an intercultural dialogue and explore the multiplicity of meanings, resonances, connections, concerns and practices that arises from any activist piece, then we need to create a route into it which prioritizes multiplicity. Translation as a research methodology enables this type of engagement. This is significant when we occupy the position of teacher or facilitator, as students may be reluctant to engage with certain types of activist material or may see the teacher or facilitator as spokesperson and so provider of definitive insight on the material. Translation can be a route into understanding and examining cultural and activist practices with which students are unfamiliar to enable them to generate research questions as a basis for developing strategies for analysing and creating new critical insights into those practices.

In the example previously given of the performance *La caída de las campanas*, which does not take a text as a starting point, opening a discussion on translating the hashtag which accompanies it provides a way for students to critically engage with it and to begin to understand, ask questions about and critique activist performances. At the same time, this process of translation as research facilitated in a workshop generates key research questions which provide the basis for further investigation and new insights into this piece. As a result, I argue that advocating for translation as a methodology for critical inquiry which opens up intercultural dialogue is valuable and fruitful even if the final objective is not a new translation. This is because this methodology activates new types of analysis that are important as the basis for new scholarly work. This research process also challenges us to interrogate the terms that we use to analyse and discuss the performance, the issue of gender-based violence and its global repercussions. In the discussion above, I included *feminicidio* as a frame of reference which enables us to conceptualize the significance of the performance. One of the key contributions that this attention to language can offer is a route into a detailed exploration of critical terms and concepts so that we ask: how does feminicide disrupt, expand and revitalize our understanding of this phenomenon in the context we are studying and the context in which we find ourselves? As a term that arises from a specific context, but which resonates in others, how can it provide new insights into this issue as a global one? How can we apply it, translate it and build upon it?

I argue that by using translation as a research methodology for interrogating activist practice in the context of workshops, teachers and students can fruitfully explore the complex multiplicity at the heart of both translation and activism. The multiple responses and insights that this research methodology generates within a workshop context can be a powerful tool to shift the focus away from individual perspectives by enabling students to critically engage with activist practice as a way to expand their own perspective. In the workshop, we can create a space in which we generate a series of research questions, while enabling students to experiment with possible translation solutions which are informed and made possible by an awareness of multiplicity. As students trial possible translations, based on an awareness of multiplicity, they also become aware of the ways in which their own languages enable them to establish a connection to some (but probably not all) aspects of the source culture, language and practice as they encounter another culture through this process. This in itself becomes a performative act as they begin to experiment and decide how to formulate their translation. In this way, some of the characteristics of the performance material under scrutiny inform the workshop practice as students undertake performative aspects of experimentation and exploration in finding translation solutions. They might also question and explore the performative function of a hashtag itself and the role(s) that it plays in activism. The workshop, which places an emphasis on multiplicity, can offer a space in which the multiple responses to this process can occur, including experimentation with translation possibilities, generation of research questions, identifying connections to the target context. Each of these activities is underpinned by the markers of the translation workshop previously identified: shared dialogue and collaboration in working through this process. This begins to broaden students' perspective on the activist material that they are working with by fostering multiple responses and insights into the piece and dialogue about it. In the space of the workshop, multiple possible solutions can coexist and this can build students' confidence in analysing the piece and proposing translations.

In reference to theatre translation, David Johnston specifies how the translator can create intercultural 'moments of encounter on the stage' as the 'translator generates and operates within the spaces-between, in which translation engineers a cultural encounter whose defining qualities are also those of the performance: contingency, provisionality, incompleteness' (2013, p. 377). This speaks precisely to the insight into both 'here' (target) and 'there' (source) that translation, and the translation process, provide. It also specifies how the translator can actively work to establish connections between source and target cultures through their selection from within the multiple possible meanings generated by the original to enable intercultural encounter and dialogue through the performance. Therefore, Johnston signals several different possible opportunities and moments for cultural encounter during the translation process and on stage. The translation workshop outlined in this chapter is one of those opportunities through which students can encounter activist material and explore how it functions in the source and target cultures. The provisionality of these spaces-between created during the translation process is fundamental: they are generators of ideas, connections between cultures and research questions. They spark further work. They provide an essential opportunity for exploring the multiple perspectives that translation practice asks us to occupy and the ways in which a dialogue between cultures, which offers new perspectives, can be created through translation practice. In the context of a workshop, this dialogue is enacted by students and teachers or facilitators. The workshop enables us to inhabit the in-betweenness in a way which resembles Diana Taylor's description of growing up between languages:

> **Translation in this sense seems more like an evolving dialogic, citational and performatic movement, that builds on meanings and gestures, highlights the slippages and gaps, and exhausts the potentialities of silences and the unspoken to understand why some concepts, possibilities and realities come into or fall out of awareness.** (2020, p. 7)

The emphasis that Taylor places on dialogue, potentialities and the link between language and concepts are all characteristics of the translation methodology advocated here. This quotation is taken from Taylor's recent work entitled *¡Presente!: The politics of presence* (2020). The title itself is relevant to the processes and methodologies that I have outlined in this chapter. Participating by being present in a workshop which interrogates activist practice through translation as research enables us to engage with the work and the multiple meanings that it generates, as well as the concepts, cultural reference points and concerns to which it connects. But, as with the quotation from Johnston, provisionality is the marker of these in-between experiences. We are constantly in motion – never present in one location or situation for eternity – and so Taylor's reflection on multilingualism reflects how we are constantly altering our awareness of how words, ideas, concepts and perspectives relate to where we have come from and where we find ourselves now as we have multiple responses over time.

By undertaking translation processes, experimenting with words and ideas, and participating in an intercultural dialogue, we can develop a greater understanding of how knowledge is located and produced in multiple ways. This can encourage participants to decentre their own experience and develop empathy towards others.

The space of the translation workshop also offers a space in which to reflect on our current situation, where we are located and the ways in which experiencing and encountering activist practice from a different cultural context can enhance and expand our perspectives. In the translation workshop we occupy a creative space of multiplicity for a time and the awareness that we develop generates research questions which form the basis of further work, beyond the workshop itself. At the same time, the activist performances that I have examined here are also marked by their provisionality, their response and force at a particular moment in time. Translation as a process of research into activist practice enables us to recognize both the temporariness of performance and hashtags and the way they function in the present time. This process also opens up ways for us to investigate and specify how these time-specific, often site-specific, interventions of activism through performance seek to enact and envisage a future where gender-based violence is eradicated, in dialogue with the work of scholars such as Fuentes. In this way, we can specify how activism through art speaks simultaneously about multiple times, and through translation we can enable it to expand our perspectives for the future.

Conclusion

To return to the case study that I offered, how might we translate *#TocanAUnaTocanATodas* to accompany *La caída de las campanas*? The answer, of course, is that there are many possibilities, but the process of research detailed in this chapter makes us aware of the multiplicity of meanings generated by this short text, the connections it forms with other activist works, and how it links to acts of embodiment in the present and envisioned futures. As teacher-translator-academic, we can advocate for translation as a methodology for researching activist practice in a workshop setting as a way to explore multiplicity, facilitate dialogue and create spaces for intercultural encounters which have the capacity to shape new perspectives. This approach decentres our own and students' experience and challenges us to expand our understanding by establishing connections between cultures and contexts through activist performances. By taking close engagement with language as a starting point, generating research questions and then pursuing these research questions further, we can generate new scholarly insights into activist performance and practice. The workshop setting as a space in between allows us to create intercultural dialogue, embody and experiment with translation possibilities, and develop research questions. The workshop activates knowledge of words and different worlds, as well as of concepts and ideas which can challenge students to expand their perspectives. In the case of activist performance, like in the case studies provided in this chapter, the study of the relationship between language and concepts also becomes a study of the ways in which these are embodied through performance. It enables students to envisage how these become theorized and enlivened through activist interventions and how translation as research plays a role in extending the resonances of these interventions.

The research underpinning this chapter was supported in its early stages by funding from the Arts and Humanities Research Council-funded project *Language Acts and Worldmaking*. It was then developed through a grant from the Leverhulme Trust.

References

Calder, A. (1943) A propos of measuring a mobile, in unpublished manuscript, Calder Foundation archives. Accessed at *Calder–Picasso* (2019) [Exhibition]. Musée national Picasso-Paris, Paris, France, 19 February–25 August 2019.

Davis, L. (2021) *Essays Two*. London: Hamish Hamilton.

Finnegan, N. (2021) Translating narratives of sexual violence in Latin America, 66th Annual Association of Hispanists of Great Britain and Ireland, Online Conference, University College Dublin. Available from: https://www.youtube.com/watch?v=gBHEWd1J3cA (Accessed: 1 March 2023).

Fregoso, R. and Bejarano, C. (eds) (2010) *Terrorizing Women: Feminicide in the Americas*. Durham, NC: Duke University Press.

Fuentes, M. A. (2019) #NiUnaMenos (#NotOneWomanLess): Hashtag performativity, memory, and direct action against gender violence in Argentina, in Altinay, A. G. *et al.* (eds), *Women Mobilizing Memory*. New York: Columbia University Press, pp. 172–91.

Johnston, D. (2013) Professing translation: The acts-in-between. *Target*, 25 (3), 365–84. DOI: 10.1075/target.25.3.04joh.

Pavis, P. (1992) *Theatre at the Crossroads of Culture*. Trans. L. Kruger. London: Routledge.

Rossi, C. (2018) Literary translation and disciplinary boundaries: Creative writing and interdisciplinarity, in Washbourne, K. and Wyke, B. V. (eds), *The Routledge Handbook of Literary Translation*. New York: Taylor & Francis Group, pp. 42–57.

Stevens, S. (2020) Disrupting narratives of gender violence: Hekatherina Delgado and performing *La caída de las campanas* in Uruguay. *Symposium: A Quarterly Journal in Modern Literatures*, 74 (4), 191–204. DOI: 10.1080/00397709.2020.1819585.

Taylor, D. (2020) *¡Presente! The politics of presence*. Durham, NC: Duke University Press.

7

Translators Aloud: advocating for translation, translations and translators

Katie Brown, Charlotte Coombe and Tina Kover

Overview

Translators Aloud is a YouTube channel hosting videos of translators reading from their work, whether published or seeking a publisher. The channel was started by translators Charlotte Coombe and Tina Kover in May 2020 and now has over 420 videos, featuring more than 300 translators reading their translations from or into 45 different languages. As of February 2023, the channel has 1,900 YouTube subscribers and has received more than 100,000 views. Katie Brown spoke to Charlotte and Tina about how Translators Aloud began, their aims for the project and what advocacy means to them.

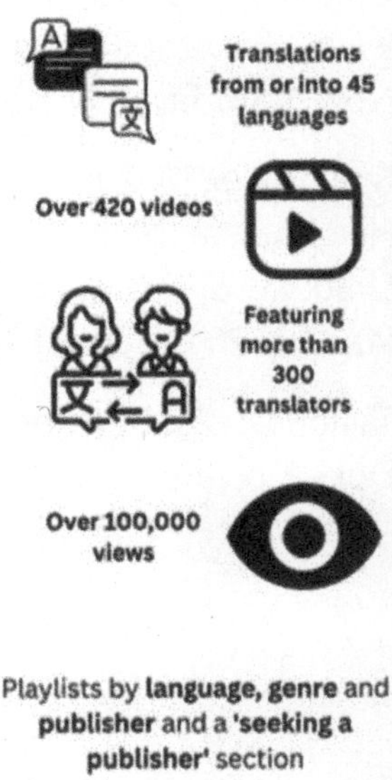

Interview

KB: We are very interested in Translators Aloud in terms of how you are simultaneously raising the profile of translation, as an activity, and of individual translators, publishers and translated works. Where did the project come from and what inspired you?

CC: It started as a lockdown project, on Twitter.

TK: I just put it out there, wondering if anybody would be interested in watching me read from one of my translations. There was an immediate, enthusiastic response, with other translators saying that they had often wondered the same thing or that they would love to see readings by translators. We set up the channel that day, Charlie and I. We'd never met, but by the end of the day we were partners.

CC: Within a few days we had a name and set up the channel and an email account. I was so surprised that something like this didn't exist for literary translations. Everyone was. Translators are often quite hesitant to promote their own work, so it seemed to feed a niche in the market.

TK: That was the first real surprise, the fact that there was nothing remotely like this. It seems like such an obvious lacuna in the translation sphere. The next revelation – which was a really great one – was how much of a hunger there was for this sort of thing.

CC: We've been putting up at least two videos a week every week since we started, if not more. We've been doing feature weeks of 15 videos a week. Sometimes [we ask ourselves], 'What if we don't get any submissions?', but it has just been constant. We've provided this platform and now we're getting to know all these translators from other languages, it's really lovely.

KB: Translators Aloud features playlists for publishers, as well as for languages. How do you see the role of publishers in advocating for translations?

TK: Small presses have played such an important role in translation becoming more visible in the last 10 or 15 years. Advocating for them, especially the ones that publish only work in translation, is just as important as advocating for individual translators. It's all interconnected.

KB: Yes, small presses are leading the way with recognizing their translators and involving them in publicity for their books.

CC: It's still quite mind-boggling when a new book comes out by, say, a Spanish author and you struggle to find online who translated it. A reader who picks it off the shelf would have no idea. It needs to change. I'm a big advocate of the 'Name the Translator' movement.

KB: One of the great things about Translators Aloud is that you don't just name the translator but we see the translator, we get to know them as a person. Do you think that seeing the translator read their work, in their own voice, with their own intonations, helps to build a sense of trust in the translator's interpretation of the text and their rewriting of it?

CC: Absolutely. Two people could translate the same book and it could be completely different. It's really important to recognize that you're a creative in your own right, putting your stamp on something. And that's a good thing.

TK: It's a wonderful thing. It's an enrichment.

CC: Every time that text finds a new life through new eyes, that's the joy of it. We've had so many comments from people saying, 'It's so nice to see the living, breathing translator who did this text.'

TK: When you watch these videos, the passion comes through so clearly. You read your own words aloud differently than you read someone else's, there's a love and a passion that comes through. Hearing somebody read the beginning of a book has the ability to draw you in; just picking up that same book and reading it to yourself wouldn't have the same impact. There is something very magnetic about having your first exposure to a text in that way.

KB: And that works for texts seeking a publisher too.

CC: If you're writing a pitch to a publisher, it's such a nice inclusion to have a link to the reading. Literary agents and publishers get loads of texts on their desk, it's so nice to be able to watch that person bringing that book alive.

TK: People put a lot of effort into these videos. They put together beautiful presentations.

CC: One of our tasks for Translators Aloud is pushing the 'Seeking a Publisher' playlist, making it better known to publishers, agents and scouts. We want this to be a go-to place for people to discover new voices from other countries and potentially bring those to English. Translators play a central role in the publishing process and so many people don't understand that still. We're here shouting, 'We've got great books for you!' We've all got books burning a hole in our back pocket that we're desperate to translate. Ask us what we're working on.

TK: One of the things that we're working to counteract is not just the tendency of larger publishers or the reading public to overlook the contribution of translation but the tendency that many translators themselves have to be extremely self-effacing, to downplay their own role in the world of publishing and as creative artists. When we reach out to translators to ask for a reading, a lot of times there's an instinctive, 'Oh no, I couldn't.' Sometimes it's just shyness, but other times it's because we're so used to being pushed into the background. You start to think that's the way it should be and it seems almost wrong when somebody says, 'We want to shine the spotlight right on you.' It's about going beyond preaching to the choir. We do want to be a repository for scouts and agents, but also for people who wouldn't normally read work in translation or actively seek it out. We want to say that this is all just really good literature. We also want the channel to be a pedagogical tool, for students of languages and of world literature. We want to include more essay videos of translators talking about their work.

KB: Another way in which you support translation and translators is through selling merchandise to fund a full bursary for a Black, Asian or ethnically diverse literary translator from anywhere in the world to attend the BCLT Summer School. Where did this idea come from and how is it going?

TK: From early on, we wanted to do something like that. It became very apparent within the first few months of having the channel that literary translators are mostly white. Seeing it brought it home visually.

CC: We have fundraised for the BCLT and they will be in charge of selecting a recipient of the bursary. We aim to do it every year if we can make enough funds. We'll hopefully do a feature with this year's scholar and get them to read from a project they're working on. We want the channel to support emerging translators. Translation can feel very isolating, especially when you're trying to get established. I hope seeing all those faces on the channel is never intimidating to newcomers; I hope it feels supportive. When you're starting out in translation, one of the main things is making yourself known to people, otherwise they might not feel confident to trust you with a project. Appearing on the channel is a way of saying, 'Here I am. I'm a literary translator, look at what I can do.'

TK: We did a collaboration with the Stephen Spender Trust [which hosts an annual poetry translation competition for schools as well as open category entrants]. All of the winners and honourable mentions in all the different age categories read their translations. That was brilliant and hopefully the beginning of a lifelong love of this work. Translation is for everybody; there's no age too early to start taking an interest.

KB: What does 'translation and advocacy' mean to you, both in your role running Translators Aloud and as translators?

TK: In my role as a translator, what my work has always been about to an extent, and is becoming more and more about, is amplifying the voices of people who may not otherwise reach a broad enough audience, whether that means marginalized communities, migrant communities, or women in countries and regions where female voices are not heard as much as they should be. That's always been a huge privilege. I definitely do consider that advocacy. Advocacy can take many forms, but in the world of literature, this is one of the most important forms it can take. Translators are champions of underrepresented voices globally. We also advocate for translators. With Translators Aloud, we're doing what we can to give translators a louder voice as fully recognized and acknowledged creative professionals.

CC: You don't always get to choose what you translate. Sometimes it is a struggle to get the smaller voices out when the publisher doesn't want it or doesn't think it will sell, so you're always working hard to get these books into the hands of the right editors who will see the importance of it. Supporting others in our industry, getting our names on the covers, getting appropriate royalties, not settling for less – advocating for all of those things is something more and more translators are getting involved with.

KB: That fits with the shift away from seeing translation only as an activity for the independently wealthy.

CC: It's a big debate. There is this issue around translation where some people see it as something you do just for the love of it, whereas most translators I know are trying

> to make a living from it or activities related to it. But you can't force people to push for higher rates, especially when they're starting out and trying to get that first break. It's a thorny issue, but there needs to be much more transparency and a push for fairer and higher rates for translation. The more we can support each other, the stronger we are.

Search for 'Translators Aloud' on YouTube or follow @LoudTranslators on Twitter.

Afterword: spaces for translation as research, practice and advocacy

Catherine Boyle

Overview

This afterword reflects on the work of translation as a pathway to the potential for community-making and to 'connect[ing] specialized knowledge with the everyday life-world' (Spellmeyer, 2003, p. 22). Translation is built on the impetus of an initial act of trust: that what we aim to translate will find a new home, a new set of interlocutors, a new audience, land anew in a different place. Inevitably, the subjectivity of the translator comes into play, given the initial singular nature of the process, but this subjectivity is not singular. It is located in a community, in assumptions, beliefs, a view of the status quo, an imagined construction of the landscape into which the newly translated piece will be received. The translator, in many ways, makes informed guesses that they have to defend and rethink as they guide the new work into its possible new home. Through looking at one experience of developing an environment for translation and thinking of the role of the university, these final reflections on advocacy shine a light on translation as an experimental space with the capacity to provide the freedom to test and propose new works, ideas and ways of worldmaking.

Learning from experience: an emblematic case study

Out of the Wings started in 2008 as a research project funded by the Arts and Humanities Research Council (AHRC), with the rather more unwieldy title of 'Spanish and Spanish American Theatres in Translation. A Virtual Environment for Research and Practice'. The principal aim was to enhance the awareness of the rich and immensely varied world of theatre in Spanish, spanning from the theatre of the 'Golden Age' of seventeenth-century Spain to the most recent work from Spain and Spanish America. Translation has always been a means of sharing great dramatic writing and was the natural heart of the project: the virtual environment that remains online is a repository of 'details of plays written in Spanish in different periods and countries, as well as information about their authors, sample translations into English, synopses, performance histories and many other tools for interpreting the featured drama'.[1] Out of the Wings also aimed to create community by bringing together the multiple groups that make theatre happen, by engaging researchers, teachers and younger learners through methods that were intended to be exportable. That is, they could be easily taken up and used in relation to other forms of translation and other languages.

What has come to be known as the Out of the Wings Collective began in 2015, after the funded period of the project. It was a way of continuing the work of advocacy for the task of translators and was a meeting place for those drawn to the idea of translation as a collective and community-making enterprise, one that crossed the still-complex boundaries of the academic, the creative and the practical. The method was, and continues to be, simple. We gather on the last Friday of every month to share a new translation of a play from Spanish or Portuguese (and, increasingly, other languages of the global Iberian world) by reading the entire play and discussing

[1] See the Out of the Wings website: **https://outofthewings.org/**. The initial project was jointly led by Catherine Boyle (King's College London), David Johnston (Queen's University Belfast), Jonathan Thacker (Oxford University) and Paul Spence (King's College London), with postdoctoral researchers Gwynneth Dowling, Gwen MacKeith and Kathleen Jeffs and PhD researcher John O'Neill.

it. These monthly table reads – the casts are whoever joins us in person or online – provide the opportunity to share different stages of translation, to consider questions of, for example, cultural transfer, register, tone, understanding, to share advice about where a play might go next and imagine that next step, including how to advocate for the work, how it might land and be received in the different environments of our participants. From a group configured by about ten academic researchers, PhD students, translators and theatre practitioners, we have grown to an international community of around 300 members. We have read around 95 new translations, have held seven annual festivals of theatre in translation that have showcased 38 plays in rehearsed readings, which, since 2019, have been published with Inti Press.[2] The key point here is that Out of the Wings has grown to be a place for advocacy. It has achieved the aim of being a multiple space, that is, one in which people find room for different interests and ambitions and outcomes in an environment that is often isolating with institutions that are hard to reach. An easy diagram illustrates the interests and reach of the collective, all interconnected, with different members working in one or more areas.

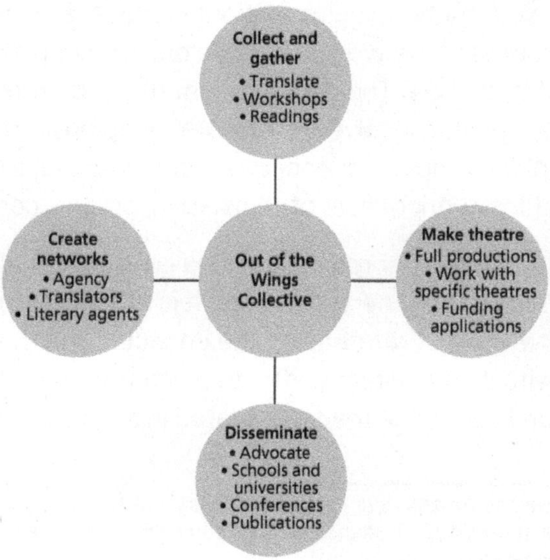

Figure 4. Examples of the interconnected work of the Out of the Wings Collective

[2] For a list of plays read since 2015, see **https://ootwfestival.com/archive/**. For information about Inti Press, see **https://www.intipress.com/**.

Increasingly, Out of the Wings is a model for other translation collectives. We, in turn, are informed by and advocate for different models of engagement and environment building. On a personal note, a major reference point is the multifaceted theatre environment developed in Chile around the university theatre, where practitioners' work prompts responses from, for example, literary writers, political scientists, psychoanalysts and literary theorists to develop an understanding of the place theatre (and, by extension, other arts) occupies as a social and cultural agent in the context of change.[3] In one table read in 2016, we heard from a Mexican author about the Festival Internacional de Teatro Universitario (FITU, International Festival of University Theatre) of the Universidad Nacional Autónoma de México (UNAM, Autonomous National University of Mexico).[4] The festival's aims – to foment and disseminate the innovative productions, practice and values of university theatre – became the model for our first sharing / *muestra* / *mostra* of plays in translation from the Global Iberian world: five plays by five female dramatists from five different countries on five nights.[5] Bringing these ideas and methodologies into our practice is an act of translation that sets the work in a broad economy of intellectual and creative exchange. The development of our community of translation advocates involved, therefore, bringing across practice from other places and experiences, encouraging the potentially transformational work of acts of translation, broadly conceived.

The trajectory can be unpredictable. This is a space that is, inevitably, marked by time and events. It is difficult to speak about anything now without referencing the impact of the Covid-19 pandemic with its devastating effects on community. We had, from early on in our table reads, operated in a hybrid form (the

---

[3] As an example, the *Revista Apuntes de Teatro* has played a central role since the 1960s in documenting Chilean theatre. For further information, see **https://revistaapuntes.uc.cl/**.
[4] For information on the Festival Internacional de Teatro Universitario, see **https://teatrounam.com.mx/teatro/entradasteatro/convocatoria-2023-30o-festival-internacional-de-teatro-universitario/**.
[5] For information about the first outing of what became the Out of the Wings Festival, see **https://ootwweb.wordpress.com/**.

term 'hybrid' not yet being part of our daily lexicon). At that time, our artisanal hybrid form was a way of keeping close any collaborators who had moved away and then became a way of bringing in new members. During the pandemic, the last Friday of every month became a more urgent date in the diary, a moment of community and recognition in our isolating worlds. Barbara Fuchs refers to the online theatre space as moving from seeming like a 'quick fix' to being 'hugely enabling – not just a life raft but a flotilla of rapidly proliferating possibilities' (Fuchs, 2022, p. 1). In rethinking our practice, we joined the pandemic world and went fully online, 'collaborating across the globe' (Fuchs, 2022, p.11), occupying and navigating the form of presentation via the Zoom window, to continue the work of translation as a criss-crossing system of encounter, misencounter and discovery in these new contact zones that had been thrust upon us.

In a forum that immediately predated the pandemic we asked attendees to complete the sentence, 'I belong to the Out of the Wings Collective because…'. The aim was to offer potential new members an understanding of the ways in which diverse individual goals and ambitions can live within a creative enterprise and to convince people that what we do can be translated to other environments. The collective, we heard, is a space for networking, for meeting people who want to translate and share experience; a place where translators test work; an opportunity to respond to questions and comments and use these to move work forward, including to full production; a generous and open space where we learn from each other; a chance to move into and out of the languages we know; a place to explore the complexity of otherness.

It is the case that an overarching goal or dream, in the field of theatre translation, might be full production in a major theatre venue. Yet there is a very slim chance of that happening, given the dearth of professional productions of new translated theatre. Throughout Out of the Wings symposiums, conferences and conversations, and way beyond, certain questions haunt the air: why should Spanish- and Portuguese-language theatre have more space than other 'non-English' theatres? Why should these theatres take up the space of local dramatists writing in English? Many conversations over many years have the question of potential (and dismay) at their heart: why don't the major theatres in the UK take translation more seriously, move beyond the well-known authors adopted into our canon – for example, Chekhov, Ibsen, Lorca.[6] Plays whose difference has so often been eradicated through a process of naturalization, through lack of engagement with the original, through the material force of the market: how, for example, to sell another *The House of Bernarda Alba* (Federico García Lorca) other than to suggest that it has been made more radical?[7] Yet, in this environment, sticking to the goal of the major production limits our vision of what is actually being generated by the many spaces for translation that have been growing over the years. What is clear is that advocacy through translation takes many shapes. If we limit ourselves to one goal, we lose the breadth, depth and opportunity that translation and collective enterprise offer.

Work in translation is often about vying for space. As we make the case for the plays we translate, we have to acknowledge that we are advocating alongside many others, including local playwrights trying to access the same theatre spaces. And in vying for these spaces, our efforts beg the very practical question of what purpose a new foreign play serves when 'we' already have perfectly good, or perhaps even better, home-grown ones. Over the years of working with Out of the Wings, these questions have changed and become more complex. We have joined many other practitioners in creating our own, smaller, spaces for translation. One such space is that of the rehearsed reading (which forms the basis of our festival). It is ephemeral: a short (at most two days) rehearsal period with a director and group of actors,

---

[6] For fuller discussions about the environment for theatre translation, see David Johnston, *Stages of Translation* (1996); Carole-Anne Upton, *Moving Target* (2000); Geraldine Brodie and Emma Cole, *Adapting Translation for the Stage* (2017); Geraldine Brodie, *The Translator on Stage* (2018).

[7] See the advertising for *The House of Bernarda Alba* at the National Theatre, London, 2023.

involving an encounter with a new play from a different culture and language, a rehearsed reading, script in hand, in front of an audience, a fleeting moment of achievement and the desire to carry on exploring the new world into which we have been invited. And then, usually, nothing. And yet, something has happened; people have come together in a type of pop-up community. Words, poetry, ideas, difference, imagination, challenge have occupied the room. Perhaps someone will share this experience with someone else, or another group. This space of the reading brings into sharp relief immediate questions of relevance and social reach, intensely related to our here and now. Because of its pared-down form, the reading highlights, for example, the question of voice, of English as a multilingual language, mediated by Englishes from all over the world and by languages from which speakers learn the language: multiple forms of articulating the subjective and individual within the collective experience. In multicultural and multilingual environments, the question of who 'we' are and what 'local' is evolves. As David Johnston says, rehearsed readings 'present the opportunity to encourage audiences to look outwards from their own cultural matrix, imagining alternative ways of understanding of their own position in time and space' (2017, p. 98).

The orthodoxy of translating into one's native language has become more fluid. The speaking of the translations is no longer the property of the native speaker and so the role of the rehearsed reading changes. A reading might previously have had the undertone of hearing the play as if it were written in English and assessing the linguistic performability of the text. When a writer is translating into a second language, cadences might be transferred through rhythm and sentence structure, tag words appear, idioms rendered into something that might not sit neatly in the 'native' ear. And so, natural distancing and estranging effects might be more present. That the play – or any translated piece – is from elsewhere cannot be denied. This is part of the renewal of the receiving language, through subtle shifts in speaking and hearing, previously unknown words crossing the air of the auditorium. In Out of the Wings discussions, we return to these questions insistently because translation demands that we do; we are moving with the voices of the original play, the original authors. When these voices land in the new place of production, they meet, for example in the UK context, the complexity of accent, region, class, received pronunciation, access to being heard. Who has the right to speak? For whom? To whom? Who has the right to speak up and be heard in English? For whom can we speak? How? These are questions of language and so of socio-political power, of identity politics, of inclusion, of human rights. This aspect of advocating is important because we are part of international and multilingual communities of translators working to bring narratives and voices to diverse audiences. This process becomes, then, advocacy for inclusivity in casting and performance, As Claire Syler says in relation to US casting practice, open approaches to casting and representation on stage are 'a way to invite more people to the table so that the full breadth of US identities can be reflected onstage' (Syler and Banks, 2019, p. 4). Participation in a collective enterprise can provide the energy and confidence to reach new, independent spaces and so translation becomes generative of social potential.

What is clear to me is that what we need to do is to keep on creating spaces and possibilities, with the goal that we create moments of contact and of hopefulness: translation zones in all senses. This takes the form of the creation of spaces for experimenting and testing what we have trusted we can transfer across language, time and space. The spaces that we create are ones where we test our object of transfer, what George Steiner calls our initiative trust, the leap of faith through which we intuit that 'there is "something there" to be understood, that the transfer will not be void' (1998, p. 312). The rehearsed reading is the place where we collectively challenge the possibility that our trust is not the whole process, that a new home can be found. This is about the intent of the venturing into and out of Steiner's hermeneutic trust. In the academy, it might mean that we are willing to teach a piece, that we think it will stand up to interrogation in the classroom and through a series of recognized literary modes of interpretation; our way of making literature and of creating the literary canon through teaching and engagement with colleagues and students. In the realm of theatre translation, it means embodying it, walking with it as a type of go-between. In the process we develop research as practice and praxis: 'doing, reflecting, reading, articulating, doing' (Nelson, 2013, p. 32). Nelson goes on: 'This is also a process of demystification: of the exclusive knowledge and research privilege of the academic; of the exalted exclusivity of the artists' way of seeing and doing that which nobody else understands' (p. 32). While the spaces created by our reading may not (immediately) lead to major productions, they play an important role in defying known structures of knowledge, questioning what is accepted as research and, more importantly, poking at and challenging the closed worlds of meaning around which so much of our cultural production prowls, to paraphrase Derrida (2002).

Language Acts and Worldmaking is quintessentially a place for advocacy. In accordance with the demands of the Open World Research Initiative (OWRI), of which it is part, this is advocating for language learning, for research and for the place of the arts and humanities in our universities and societies. It has been a space for militating against the lexicon of crisis in the sector, confounded by economic models that cannot deal with creative production as intrinsically related to the role of universities in developing skills and training. Worldmaking is about how we make and remake our world through language, how the historic materiality of language is in a constant process of reinvention, in which translation plays a pivotal role. As Lawrence Venuti says:

> Translation is in fact basic to human cognition, active in the pursuit of intelligibility and in the negotiation of linguistic and cultural differences. It can facilitate or obstruct communication, sometimes simultaneously. Yet insofar as issues of cosmopolitanism, globalization and transnationalism have become persistent themes in humanistic study, the urgency to recognize translation as a key practice of intercultural communication has never been greater. (Venuti, 2017, p. 11)

During the Covid-19 pandemic, the project 'Worldmaking in the Time of Covid-19' brought language students together to provide access to the variety of global experiences and to the different approaches. A key goal was to take us forcefully out of the experience and narratives dominant narratives in the UK, to enact the translators' sophisticated awareness of otherness as a form of understanding, of examining how we 'report' and 'remake' the worlds around us, to use Nelson Goodman's formulation (1978, p. 22). These projects and their reach have been made possible by the university space, by grants and funding bodies within a privileged environment. The university space is one that can facilitate working with many different partners, all engaged in communities where the negotiation of language difference is part of daily life.[8] Working with different partners is about invitation and trust, about the complex dynamics of hospitality. There is a language of welcome that is available to all and that translation facilitates.

All translation is advocacy, all translation opens our imagination to the known and unknown, to make the insecurity and instability of crossing part of the way we look out on the world. As Rebecca Walkowitz says, it is important to think about how 'to experience both fluency and lack of fluency' (2022, p. 949). The translation practices shared here grow from the university space, understood as a 'communications hub' with the potential to 'circulate existing knowledge in unprecedented ways' (Spellmeyer, 2003, p. 23). Our practice seeks to generate new interventions from the multiple places of language production and exchange to reach into our classrooms and our engagement beyond the academy in community building that recognizes processes of exchange that become pathways to opening the imagination and to active engagement beyond the small spaces we occupy as individuals.

---

[8] See Ana Aguiar de Medeiros and Debra Kelly, *Language and Hospitality in Worldmaking: How languages act in the world* (2022), pp. 102–27.

References

Aguiar de Medeiros, A. and Kelly, D. (2022) Language and hospitality in worldmaking: How languages act in the world, in Boyle C. and Kelly D. (eds), *Language Acts and Worldmaking. How and why the languages we use shape our world and lives.* London: John Murray Learning, pp. 102–27.

Brodie, G. (2018) *The Translator on Stage.* London: Bloomsbury.

Brodie, G. and Cole, E. (eds) (2017) *Adapting Translation for the Stage.* London and New York: Routledge.

Derrida, J. (2002) What is a 'relevant' translation?, in Venuti, L. (ed), *The Translation Studies Reader.* London and New York: Routledge, pp. 423–46.

Fuchs, B. (2022) *Theater of Lockdown: Digital and distanced performance in a time of pandemic.* London: Methuen Drama.

Goodman, N. (1978) *Ways of Worldmaking.* Indianapolis, IN: Hackett Publishing Company.

Johnston, D. (ed) (1996) *Stages of Translation.* London: Absolute Classics.

Johnston, D. (2017) Teaching theatre translation, in Venuti, L. (ed.), *Teaching Translation.* London and New York: Routledge, pp. 94–101.

Nelson, R. (2013) *Practice as Research in the Arts.* London: Palgrave Macmillan.

Spellmeyer, K. (2003) *Arts of Living. Reinventing the humanities for the twenty-first century.* New York: State University of New York Press.

Steiner, G. (1998) *After Babel: Aspects of language and translation* (3rd edn). Oxford: Oxford University Press.

Syler, C. and Banks, D. (2019) *Casting a Movement: The Welcome Table initiative.* London and New York: Routledge.

Upton, C.-A. (ed) (2000) *Moving Target: Theatre translation and cultural relocation*. Manchester, UK, and Northampton, MA: St. Jerome Publishing.

Venuti, L. (ed) (2017) *Teaching Translation*. London and New York: Routledge.

Walkowitz, R. (2022) English as an additional language. *PMLA*, 137 (5), 926–34.

Index

About the contributors

Tom Boll is Associate Professor in Literary Translation at the University of East Anglia where he curates the translation collection in the British Archive for Contemporary Writing. He is the author of *Octavio Paz and T.S. Eliot: Modern Poetry and the Translation of Influence* (Legenda, 2012). His translation of Jorge Luis Borges and Osvaldo Ferrari's *Conversations, Volume 2* was published by Seagull Books in 2015. He is currently working on a book about translators' papers in the archive for Routledge.

Catherine Boyle is Professor of Latin American Cultural Studies. Since 2008 she has directed the Out of the Wings project, dedicated to theatre translation, research and performance, and since 2018 she has been director of *Language Acts and Worldmaking*. She has published widely on Latin American cultural and gender studies and has translated theatre, poetry and prose, including Sor Juana Inés de la Cruz (Mexico), Andrés Kalawski (Chile), Juan Radrigán (Chile) and Mariano Tenconi Blanco (Argentina). A recent translation is *Inventario para despues de la guerra / Inventory for after the War* by Venezuelan writer Raquel Rivas Rojas, published by La cartonera editions in Santiago de Chile (2022).

Katie Brown is Senior Lecturer in Latin American Studies at the University of Exeter. Her current work focuses on the intersections of migration, publishing and translation, with a particular interest in contemporary Venezuela. She is author of *Writing and the Revolution: Venezuelan Metafiction (2004–2012)*, published by Liverpool University Press in 2019. Katie teaches translation at undergraduate and MA levels and is a founding member of the transatlantic translation collective *Colaboratorio Ávila*. Her translation of *Desde la salvajada* by Alejandra Banca is forthcoming.

Charlotte Coombe is an award-winning British translator working from French and Spanish into English since 2008, across a variety of genres including literary fiction and non-fiction. She has translated around a dozen books by authors including Marvel Moreno, Margarita García Robayo, Ricardo Romero, Eduardo Berti, Vincent Doumeizel and Abnousse Shalmani. Her translations of short stories and poetry have appeared in literary journals such as *Asymptote, The Southern Review, Modern Poetry in Translation, World Literature Today* and

Words without Borders. She is also the co-founder of Translators Aloud, a YouTube project that shines a light on translators reading from their work.

Beverley Costa is a psychotherapist. In 2000 she set up the Mothertongue multi-ethnic counselling service for multilingual clients. In 2009 she set up a mental health interpreting service and in 2010 she established the national Bilingual Therapist and Mental Health Interpreter Forum. She founded the Pásalo Project www.pasaloproject.org in 2017 to disseminate learning from Mothertongue. She is a Senior Practitioner Fellow at Birkbeck, University of London and a Senior Visiting Research Fellow at the University of Reading. Her book *Other Tongues: Psychological therapies in a multilingual world* was published in 2020.

Tina Kover is the translator of more than 30 books from French. Her work has won the Albertine Prize, the French Voices Award and the Lambda Literary Award and has been shortlisted for the (US) National Book Award, the International Dublin Literary Award, the PEN Translation Prize, the Warwick Prize for Women in Translation, the Oxford-Weidenfeld Translation Prize and the Scott Moncrieff Prize. She leads literary translation workshops for the American Literary Translators Association and masterclasses in literary translation for Durham University. She is also the co-founder of Translators Aloud, a YouTube channel that features literary translators reading from their own work.

Sarah Maitland is Senior Lecturer in Translation Studies at Goldsmiths, University of London, where she leads the MA in Translation and the PhD programmes in Translation and Translation by Practice. She is Deputy Editor of the *Journal of Specialised Translation* and until 2021 was an elected member of the Executive Council of the International Association for Translation and Intercultural Studies (IATIS). Sarah is author of *What Is Cultural Translation?* (2017), published by Bloomsbury Academic, as well as numerous works on translation theory and practice. As a professional translator, she specializes in creative translation services, with a focus on stage and screen.

Teresa Murjas is Professor in Theatre and Performance at the University of Reading, where she also holds the roles of Academic Champion for Public Engagement with Research and Impact Lead. Her practice-led, intermedial work includes the translation and staging of late nineteenth- and early twentieth-century Polish-language drama and, more recently, extensive collaboration with heritage-sector organizations on projects that creatively animate a broad range of archives and collections.

Sophie Stevens is Lecturer in Latin American and Caribbean Studies at the Institute of Languages, Cultures and Societies, University of London. She is a researcher, theatre translator and practitioner and completed a Leverhulme Early Career Fellowship in the School of Literature, Drama and Creative Writing at the University of East Anglia in 2023. Her research investigates the work of Latin American women dramatists in order to explore links between activism, performance, digital networking and translation. Through this work she advocates for an interdisciplinary approach to Modern Languages teaching. She is an Associate Researcher on the *Language Acts and Worldmaking* project and a member of the Out of the Wings Collective. Her monograph *Uruguayan Theatre in Translation: Theory and Practice* was published by Legenda in 2022.

Lisha Xu is currently a Teaching Fellow in Chinese and Translation Studies at the School of Literatures, Languages and Cultures at the University of Edinburgh. Her research interests are in theatre translation and literary translation in general, especially translating *xiqu* for the anglophone stage and the study of Chinese translators of the early twentieth-century diaspora. She has recently published in the Special Issue on Translation and Performance Cultures of *Translation Studies*. She has been commissioned to co-edit a special issue of *JoSTrans* on theatre translation, to be published in 2024/25, and is currently preparing a research monograph on the topic of translating classical Chinese opera.